J. R. S. (James Robert Soda) Pitts

Life and bloody Career of the executed Criminal, James Copeland,

the great Southern Land Pirate

J. R. S. (James Robert Soda) Pitts

**Life and bloody Career of the executed Criminal, James Copeland, the great Southern Land Pirate**

ISBN/EAN: 9783743314955

Manufactured in Europe, USA, Canada, Australia, Japa

Cover: Foto ©ninafisch / pixelio.de

Manufactured and distributed by brebook publishing software (www.brebook.com)

J. R. S. (James Robert Soda) Pitts

# Life and bloody Career of the executed Criminal, James Copeland, the great Southern Land Pirate

# MEMOIR OF THE AUTHOR.

The author of the ensuing publication was born in Effingham county, Georgia. His grandfather, Dr. Soda, was a native of Cologne, an ancient city on the Rhine, in Prussia. Here educated to the science of physic, he afterwards became a practicing physician. Rather early in life, he came to the United States of America, and settled in the city of Savannah, Georgia, where the remainder of his life, some thirty years, was spent. Here, and during this time, he practiced in the medical profession with success and distinction. He married an American lady, the issue from which consisted in only one son and one daughter, Robert and Jane Rosettah.

About the year 1830, the latter, with J. G. W. Pitts, were married in the city of Savannah, Georgia. The result from this nuptial union is the existence of the "author." With him, in 1834, his parents removed from Georgia to Rankin county, near Brandon, Mississippi; but the wife and mother did not long survive afterward, as will be seen from the following record found in the family Bible:

"Mrs. Jane Rosettah Pitts, wife of J. G. W. Pitts, departed this life the 7th day of January, A D., 1835, in the 21st year of her age, after severely suffering under a complicated disease of two years' standing, which baffled the skill of the best physicians."

The author was left an orphan at a very early age—only two years old. He was consigned over to the guardian care of an affectionate grandmother, who performed the charge both creditably to herself and in perfect accord with the welfare of the infant entrusted to her charge.

He was sent to school as early as convenience would permit, and, at intervals, continued until the age of twenty-one, when his friends brought him out for Sheriff of Perry county. At this period he left the school-room, and forthwith entered on the canvass, which resulted in his successful election by a handsome majority.

For some four years he continued in this office, during which time the painful duty devolved on him of executing James Copeland, the subject of the present work. Next came his memorable trial in the city of Mobile, Alabama, to answer an inveterate prosecution for libel—a trial which involved the best talent of the bar, and resulted in the conviction of the author by such means as truly gave only the shadows of victory to the straining prosecution, and triumph in real substance to the defence.

At a very early age, the author manifested a preference for the study of medicine, and in his capacity of Sheriff, his leisure hours, apart from the requirements of his office, were spent in making proficiency in his favorite science; and still more so after his trial—immediately following which he attended a medical college with ardor and assiduity, and ever since has been engaged in the practice of his profession.

# INTRODUCTION.

There is, perhaps, nothing within the sphere of human operations which more affect the present and future generations, either for good or evil, than a faithful narration of history and biography. But the effects, either for better or worse, depend pretty much on the comments and conclusions of the historian and biographer themselves. He may have an unprejudiced mind, he may chronicle the events of a nation faithfully and correctly, and he may be capable of delineating the mighty strokes and nicer shades of individual character with all the force and brilliancy which extraordinary genius can command; but if his deductions or inferences be unsound or erroneous, the effects will extend to all parts of society, both the present and the future.

For instance, and as an illustration, the poet said of Lord Bacon:

"The greatest, the wisest, and the *meanest* of mankind."

This is a forcible declaration, and one that belongs to the true philosophy which others must adopt before they can be the real benfactors of mankind. Had the poet gone further and particularized the conduct of this great man, in what consisted his exalted virtues, and wherein he has contributed so much to the benefit of after ages—giving him credit for all this, and stamping it with true glory, admiration and immortality—holding up the same as worthy of imitation for aspiring youth; and then followed by a painful portrayal of his enormous vices which have had their share in producing so much corruption and misery on society at large—making manifest, according to the declaration of another poet, that "an honest man is the noblest work of God;" and that it is far better to be honest, though humble, than to have a combination of character of all which is great and all which is mean; let it be repeated, had the poet drawn his lines in some such manner, far happier might have been the result.

Again, war is the scourge of humanity. Of all woes, there are none which can be compared to the horrors of protracted warfare. Neither tongue nor pen can adequately depict the miseries which flow in the train of consequences. The rust, disease, exposure and pestilence of camp life; the crowded hospitals of accumulated wretchedness; the sweat and smoke—the blood and groans of the red battle-field; these form but a very small part of the dire afflictions which flow from hostile collisions of this nature—to say nothing of the burdens entailed on posterity by waste of treasure—leaving an interminable debt to oppress generations yet unborn!

Here the fashionable historian has a fine field to work in. In dazzling colors he gilds and paints in profusion. He largely expatiates on the strategems, the manœuvering, and the master strokes of policy displayed by the commanding General. In matchless grandeur he draws his lines, made conspicuous by gleaming swords and bristling bayonets. He plants his thundering batteries on every eminence within the scope of vision. Now open the scenes of death and carnage. Red flashes, black smoke and leaden hail extend from every spot of falling conflict. Hand to hand, foot to foot, breast to breast. First one and then another of distinguished officers dropping, "covered all over with immortal glory." Grounds taken and retaken. One wing giving away, another pressing victoriously onward over heaps of the slain. Here stubbornly contested, then riding on the fiery wings of battle overpowering all opposition—producing route, defeat and dreadful slaughter on every road of retreat. Such animating descriptions animate other armies and other Generals. Not only is the impetuous enthusiasm of the common soldier excited, but also the ardor and emulation of the General himself. The young, the old—all seem to desire more opportunities to occur for the exercise of prowess, as well as for further demonstrations of martial glory. But it is quite possible to conceive how the historian could have produced quite a contrary effect. By degrading all that appertains to warfare, and by holding up to public scorn and indignation the brutal and hellish scenes involved for purposes of rapine, plunder or false notions of honor; by descriptions of this sort war might be held in a very different estimation to what it now is.

But is the present course of the historian's pen altogether erroneous? Perhaps not. The inordinate rapacity and selfishness of human nature must be taken into account. The overpowering propensity for conquest, might against right, must be considered. A nation extremely rich in agricultural productions, in manufacturing commodities, and in everything else pertaining to wealth, yet effeminately weak in spirit and incompetent for physical protection, will stand a poor chance against the trained hordes who prefer plunder and conquest to any other pursuit. So far, then, the historian's pen is not misapplied in keeping alive and active the bravery and martial spirit of a nation to secure its own against the unscrupulous encroachments of other nations, or against the wild infatuations of parts of the same nation.

In this department the true and correct province of the pen is to encourage, by all honorable means, bravery, magnanimity, and all other generous traits of a great nation, consistent with safety or security in the future, determined to maintain the right, and equally so not to yield anything to wrong through abject fear of consequences; at the same time favoring forbearance and exhausting all honorable means before the last resort of warfare be put in execution; while not forgetting to impress that external warfare or internal rebellion generally leave behind worse evils than those intended to be removed. A little reflection, then, must convince all of the vast and mighty influences which the historian and biographer exercise on society and nations at large, either for good or evil, according to the range or sphere occupied.

The life of the condemned criminal, James Copeland, who expiated his blood-stained career on the scaffold, together with the history of the alarming and extensive clan, which, for many long years, produced a perfect reign of terror over such a broad expanse of territory in this nation, and of which said James Copeland formed one of the principal leaders in the clan—clearly showing the causes which favored the progress, as well as the causes which produced dismemberment and final dissolution—such a life and history cannot fail, even at this late date, after so long an interval of unavoidable interruption, of materially interesting and benefitting the public at large.

James Copeland was executed in 1857. His life and the history of the clan were published in 1858. The sale of the work was progressing wonderfully when a ruinous prosecution commenced against the author in Mobile, in another State, Alabama, for libel on several parties by the names of Messrs. Overall, Moulton and Cleaveland; the former being the principal actor in this prosecution, at least overtly so. This circumstance, in connection with the crippling of the author's pecuniary resources, together with the all-absorbing questions involved in the late internal war, through which we have just passed, prevented any but the first edition from appearing, which only circulated in a very limited extent of territory.

The obstacles here referred to are now pretty much out of the way. Opportunity is offered for republication on a far broader basis than before. Time is the corrector of errors and excesses. Heated passions give way to sober reason. In the enlarged edition which will shortly appear, impartial minds will at once discover that the principal object is to do justice to all—injury to no one; but this course will not exclude the guilty from exposure, yet it will endeavor to exonorate the innocent who may have been accused through misnomer or by inadvertant mistake.

Great and influential men league together, sometimes for worthy purposes, but often for unworthy ones. It is very easy to entertain the idea that a young man just setting out in the public walks of life without the prestige of the distinguished, can easily be broken down, no matter how foully the means resorted to for accomplishment. It is strange that Governor McWillie, of the State of Mississippi, should have so tamely and willingly given up the author to the laws of another State, and more especially to the particular locality where the designing influence of the prosecutors so widely extended, while well knowing that the author could have had no motive or interest in accusing or misrepresenting any—not previously knowing anything, either of name or person, in relation to the prosecuting parties, either of good or bad—only publishing in substance the unaltered revelations as made by the convict himself, the truth of which he sealed with his last dying breath on the scaffold; and while Governor McWillie, with hundreds of others, have known from previous experience the truth of the principal particulars as related by Copeland himself. This notorious clan was not only a terror to almost every part of this State, but also of many others. But all this belongs to the past, and is only now alluded to in order to give a right understanding of all the facts and circumstances connected with the whole affair from beginning to end.

Truth and justice, by oppression and by forces foul, may be held down for awhile, but the increasing and progressive power of the springs will break and throw off the impediments—again bursting forth in vigor and strength not to be crushed nor repressed by sophistry nor by the influences of money and distinguished officials.

G. Y. Overall was the principal open prosecutor of the three.

It was clearly evinced on trial that there were other Overalls, and, to the satisfaction of the jury, it was to one of these whom Copeland referred to in his confessions; consequently, the public sentiment was in no way changed or weakened by the proceedings of the trial; but, on the contrary, was largely strengthened in favor of the substantial truths of the confessions.

Hon. P. Walker, the counsel for defense, maintained the same; and, further, that G. Y. Overall had not a shadow of right on his side for instituting the prosecution.

The author is frank to confess, from the testimony produced on trial, that G. Y. Overall established his innocence so far as he was concerned in point of time as specified in Copeland's confessions. But if this had been his only object, why not have rested satisfied with a verdict in his favor which could not have failed to have been rendered without any injury to either the author or the "confessions?" Why did he, in combination with others, resort to means so disreputable, as will afterwards be shown, to crush the author or publisher, who before did not know him, and could not have had any enmity or sordid motive against him, as well as for the purpose of destroying the "confessions," the major parts of which were well known to be strictly true? Why one part of the witnesses so infamous and in every way so suspicious? Why the strange and oscillating conduct of the Judge in varying his charges to the Jury at different stages of progress? Why, contrary to all modern usage, hold confined the jury for six long days and nights with an express and determined resolve not to release when there appeared to be no prospect of an agreement on a verdict? Why so many cunning inlets to and tampering with parts of the jury? Why, when it was worn out by fatigue and loss of rest, was the last stratagem resorted to for delusion to the effect that it was hardly worth while holding out when the penalty, if any at all, would be nothing more than a slight fine? Why the low, the despicable, and the underground agencies set at work to poison the mind of a then intended wife, and to sever the agreement of marriage which had been made in good faith on both sides? If G. Y. Overall had meant nothing more than the establishing of his own innocence as regards the confessions made, and which he unwarrantedly applied to himself, why so many mysterious forces at work and so much of corruption put in play? By endeavoring to establish too much, reaction often follows which sometimes satisfies that too little has been effected to produce any benefit to the complainer.

Public disapproval of the verdict, universal sympathy which followed the author everywhere, even within the confines of his prison—a stranger in Mobile, yet on every hand met with kind treatment both in this city and elsewhere from afar, all giving testimony against this uncalled for and malignant prosecution. Mr. Overall and company's victory was dearly bought, and left them in a far worse condition than before they commenced.

For proving too much, a miserable subterfuge was tried to make appear that Copeland was deranged, was a maniac, and his statements entirely unworthy of credit. A more signal failure could not have been attempted. If he was non compos mentis, the law grievously erred in causing his execution. Those who knew him well, those who visited him long and often in his prison, can testify to his extraordinary strength of mind. Brave and undaunted, affable in deportment, a tenacious memory, with all other indications of mental vigor, the chances are very small of making impressions touching his insanity. And all this in the face of those localities which suffered so much from the depredations of the clan, which localities can vouch for the truth of his confessions. But the jury of inquest, on an artful plea raised at the time of his trial settles this question. A man with certain death before his eyes, with not even the remotest hope of any possibility of escape, is not governed as other men are under ordinary circumstances of business and duplicity. If, to the double-dealers and the reserved, his conduct appears strange in the exposure of his associates, how much more so in the reflections on his own mother? The testimony of a dying man, given freely and without any deceptive or compulsory force, is generally considered reliable. The circumstances under which he made his confessions, having in view his fast approaching end to all earthly scenes, the internal evidences of truth which they bear, the numerous localities which can confirm the facts as in them contained, all tend to produce convictions as to the substantial accuracy of his narrations. In his last moments before the fatal drop launched him into an endless eternity, in reference, read the following certificate, correctly transcribed, as given by an eye witness in reply to an application from the author:

MOBILE, ALA., July 31st. 1873.

This is to certify that I was present at the execution of James Copeland, who was executed at Augusta, Perry county, Miss., the 30th day of October, 1857; and heard the Sheriff. J. R. S. Pitts, ask him, the said James Copeland, if the detailed history and list of names given as members of the Wages and Copeland clan were correct, and he answered the Sheriff in the affirmative that they were. T. C. CARTER.

Office 58, North Commerce st., Mobile, Ala.

Other equally reliable certificates could be given to the same effect, but the one here transcribed will suffice. The person whose signature is above given, is respectfully known pretty much throughout the City of Mobile, as well as over the greater part of Mississippi, and whose veracity none will attempt to dispute.

Let it be borne in mind that the existence of this clan continued for a great number of years, Its fields of operations extended from State to State—from shore to shore. Here murder and prodigious rapine; there burning wrecks, with hurried flights from place to place to avoid capture and the pursuits of retributive vengeance—frequently succeeding, but now and then failing for short periods of time until the reserves in men, in money, and in officials or leagued members of the bar could be brought to bear for rescue or for jail delivery by process of law. Amid all these chequered scenes of success and adversity, it would not be impossible for some unintentional errors of date to have intervened; yet, intrinsically, such errors may be of a character as not, to the smallest extent, to affect the validity or value of the "confessions" made; but still, errors of this sort, may furnish fine capital for indirect sore-headed associates to rave and foam. As a simple illustration on this point, one man saw another commit a crime on the 15th, but, on investigation, it turned out to have been done on the 16th. Now, had he stated "on or *about* the 15th," all would have been complete; but will any one contend because of the omission of this "*or about*," the whole value of the statement is destroyed?

Again, typographical errors will occur in almost all printed productions, to a greater or less extent. Such errors are sometimes insignificant and sometimes material. In the original work, as first published, some few typographical errors have been discovered. For instance, "Shonesmack" should have been Shoemake or Scheumake; but the idea of raising a fuming warfare because of such sort of errors as these, is sublimely ridiculous.

After some hesitation about propriety, the author has decided to re-publish the same as appeared in the first edition, with such few appended explanations and corrections as are necessary for distinct comprehension by the reader.

Fillial acknowledgements and a tribute of respect for the father, but mother, brothers, and associates, Copeland spared none. Without reserve—without restraint—simple and without any object of complication, truth fell fast and spontaneously during the short time he had to live. The philosopher, the statesman, and the moralist—all may deduce lessons of value to the future from his confessions. Reflections on his mother show the mighty force and influence which the female parent exercises on youth and maturity. "The rule is bad that will not work both ways." If in this case the mother produced so much of evil fruit, a contrary or an opposite one must produce contray results—hence, the vast importance of mothers both to the present and rising generations.

The Murrell clan first, then the Wages and Copeland next. Both organizations came to a tragic end. Astounding as the fact may be, there are some who prefer a life of blood and plunder and terror, to peaceful industry and the blessings of orderly society. If the life and history now under consideration should fall into the hands of some of this class, let them not indulge in the flattering unction that but for this or the other error committed, the career of the clan might have continued indefinitely. Let no such fatal delusions be cherished for a moment. Under a system of semi-civilization, where laws are only a mock farce, where amount of money is the measure of guilt or innocence; where judges on the bench, executive officials, rings, cliques, lawyers, demagogues, and even a number of the clerical order—Mr. McGrath as an instance—all operate, not according to the principles of right in consonance with the benign influences which tend towards a rule of natural order and justice, but in conformity with corrupt and sordid motives for political considerations to secure wealth and power, no matter how foul the means; under such an unhealthy condition of circumstances, organizations like the Murrell, the Wages and Copeland, however assiduously and indirectly supported by men of wealth and distinction, however bold and able the actors, cannot permanently continue. Such combinations of lawlessness for murder and plunder, incendiarism and all the other darker crimes which belong to depraved natures, must terminate in death and dissolution; but it so generally happens that the less guilty end their career on the scaffold or in some other way by the hands of an outraged community; while the higher grades of participant criminals, of larger calibre of brain, are left to revel on the spoils for which the less fortunate have had to suffer the pains of an ignominious death.

Organizations of such vast and gigantic magnitude, are incidents of a rude and transition state of society, where population is sparse, where means of protection are sadly at fault, and where so many hardened criminals make their escape through the mock forms of trials in courts, not of justice, but of ignorance and corruption under the name of liberty and a scrupulous tenderness in behalf of a spurious or false sentimental color of humanity; but in proportion as population increases, so also must detection and protection, with a better administration of law and justice increase in the same ratio, even if the forms of government have to be changed for the accomplishment of the same. Wealth cannot accumulate long without chaos and anarchy, unless protection of life and property be commensurate.

But often the closing era of such terrible organizations for bold and daring depredations on the better portions of society, then begin other organizations of less dimensions, but more dangerous, because more subtle and refined, and in every way harder of detection.

There is something terrible, or, at least, alarming in conception awakened by the names of *clans* and *bands ;* but different as regards *rings* and *cliques*. These last control legislation the executives and cabinets, and nearly the whole of the judicial rings. They are the arbiters of aspirants of every description—generally according to the price or consideration offered. But there is yet another lower grade of rings and cliques, composed of subordinate officers, picayune members of the bar, and low-down reckless strikers. When money or other sorts of gain is to be made, these strikers are set to work, and if they become involved in law difficulties, the cheap lawyers, with the assistance of the officials, are always at hand to liberate the offending culprits. Former methods of murder, conflagration and high-handed robbery have been exchanged for more intricate forms of conquest and gain.

Whoever ventures an exposure of the fashionable vices of influential circles—whoever assails the citadels and strongholds of crime and corruption, must not expect to elude numerous and deep-laid conspiracies for the sacrifice of life, which, if he escape falling a victim, he will be more than fortunate. Even so far, the author has bitterly experienced all this. The marvel is that he is yet alive and determined to continue in stronger terms than before exhibited—relying on invincible truth and the better portions of society to bear him up through the ordeal which he has to encounter. Although he has suffered much, and has had many "hair-breadth escapes" from the plots and snares laid for his destruction.

The subsequent part of the Appendix will inform the reader of several infernal concoctions for assassination when attempts at intimidation failed. The first of these will embrace particulars in the period betwixt the publication and the author's arrest, and the other about three years after the trial had terminated. The period betwixt publication and arrest cannot be devoid of interest to the reader—it is a prelude to the important trial which followed. The incidents involved during the time here referred to have ponderous bearings, in a circumstantial point of view, toward establishing the substantial correctness of Copeland's confessions, although intended to invalidate them and make a nullity of the whole.

During imprisonment Copeland seemed to fully comprehend the profound plans and commanding power of one by the name of Shoemake. This is the man who played so conspicuous a part before and on trial in combination with the three prosecuting parties of Mobile. The arch-enemy of all mankind cannot surpass him in perfidious deception.

"With smooth dissimulation well skilled to grace,
 A devil's purpose with an angel's face."

He who it was who first addressed a letter of almost matchless duplicity to the author, while residing in Perry county, under a forged or fictitious signature. He who it was who next visited the author in person, first to try the arts of persuasion, and then the designing influences of intimidation, but in either case without the desired effect. After this, he it was who entered into compact with the prosecuting three, of Mobile, bore the requisition from the Governor of Alabama to the Governor of Mississippi for the rendition of the author, and, in the circumstances connected with the arrest, acted in such a mysterious and suspicious manner as could leave no doubt that he contemplated the life of the author under a plausible pretext of resistance to lawful authority. But this object was signally defeated. A considerable number of good citizens quickly collected together, well armed for protection, and volunteered to accompany the author under arrest to Mobile, which they accordingly did, and effectually secured his safety.

The trial followed next. By careful attention to the circumstances connected with it much information may be gathered, showing the force of political considerations, and how hard the task for truth and justice, in the first efforts, to gain a triumph over a combination of wealth and intellect leagued together for bad purposes. For instance, the presiding Judge, McKinstry, could have had no personal prejudice or enmity against the author, and in his heart might have rejoiced over the dissolution of the clan, but his palpably reprehensible conduct on trial furnishes convincing evidence that he was influenced by other considerations than those of law and justice. To this fact Dr. Bevell, one of the impaneled jurymen on the case, had his eye turned in the references to the Judge's conduct and political considerations, which references will be found in his letter published in another part of the work.

On the days of trial the notorious character of this said Shoemake was made public and manifest. He was the principal witness relied on in the prosecution. Another, equally infamous, as demonstrated by the most satisfactory of testi-

C—2

mony, by the name of Bentonville Taylor, was brought from afar in rags and poverty, and sent back in costly attire with money in profusion. Does the impartial judgment require anything more to produce conviction of the shameful features of the prosecution? If so, he will find much more before he gets through the particulars of the trial. Added to this, the almost universal outburst of sympathy in behalf of the author, with letters of condolence from distant parts, all of which will be found in the proper places of the work.

Under circumstances so adverse it is not to be expected that Copeland, in his confession, could give more than a small fractional part of the transactions of the whole clan. Since then a number and variety of interesting matters have been collected from the most authentic of sources, and will be found in the appropriate place of this pamphlet.

The subject of crime opens an almost inexhaustible expanse for expatiation. An elaborate treatise on its causes and remedies is too prolix for a work of this nature—only a few passing observations on this theme will be found interspersed, which are relevant and have a direct bearing on the main topics discussed.

And now, in closing this introductory part, the author wishes the public to understand that he has no personal animosity against those who so wrongfully deprived him of his liberty, ruined him with expenses, and encompassed his life in so many intricate ways. He has not indulged in any revengeful passions, but has endeavored to strictly confine himself to the unprejudiced and impartial province of the historian and biographer—according merit where due, and with propriety denouncing crimes, corruptions and unhealthy conspiracies whenever they come in the way. And, if in so doing, he is to endure a repetition of persecutions and prosecutions, with fresh dangers added, he will try to bear them with all the fortitude he can command, with the hope that the peaceably and honestly disposed parts of the community will rally for the pulling down the edifices of vice, and for establishing a better, a purer and a healthier condition of society.

# PREFACE.

The number of years during which the Copeland and Wages Gang of Land Pirates pursued a successful career of robbery, incendiarism and murder in the United States; their final dismemberment, disgrace and violent end at the hand of retributive justice; and the stern moral lesson taught by their history and fate, have induced the undersigned to publish the confession of one of the leaders of the gang, as made by himself, in anticipation of his death at the hands of the hangman. Its accuracy may be relied on; and indeed it is hardly possible to doubt the truth of its statements, so minutely, consecutively and clearly are they related, and so consonant are they with the various localities and the characters of the men.

This confession was given to me, principally by the aid of copious memoranda which Copeland had kept for years in his diary, and which materially refreshed his memory.

James Copeland, the subject of this memoir, was born near Pascagoula river, in Jackson county, Miss., on the 18th day of January, 1823. He was the son of Isham Copeland and Rebecca Copeland, his wife—formerly Rebecca Wells. The parents had resided for many years near Pascagoula river.

Isham Copeland was a farmer in easy circumstances, with a good farm, several negroes, plenty of horses and mules and other live stock; and, in fact, he might be said to have everything about him that a family in moderate circumstances could require to enable him to live comfortably. He was the father of several sons; but, alas! this, which is by most men deemed a blessing, proved to him a curse; and after encountering many trials in youth and manhood, just when he thought to enjoy the peace and repose of old age, his son's misconduct drew on him many severe reverses of fortune, and finally drove him to the grave broken hearted.

J. R. S. PITTS.

# LIFE AND CAREER

OF

# JAMES COPELAND,

### THE SOUTHERN LAND PIRATE, AND HIS INTIMATE ASSOCIATES,

AS RELATED IN DETAIL, BY HIMSELF, IN PRISON, A FEW DAYS BEFORE HIS EXECUTION, TO DR. J. R. S. PITTS, THEN SHERIFF OF PERRY COUNTY, MISS.

---

When I was about ten or eleven years of age, my father sent me to school, and I went at intervals from time to time, to several good teachers. I might, with proper training and management, have received a liberal education. My father often insisted, and urged it upon me to study and try to obtain a good education, and he told me that he would send me to school as long as I wished to go. But being misled by my associations with bad company, I was engaged, instead, in studying mischief, and other things no way profitable to myself or advantageous to youths. It was my misfortune, that my disposition led me on to study how to cheat, defraud and swindle my comrades and school-mates, out of their pocket-knives, their money or anything they might have, which I wanted, and I was generally successful in my undertaking. If I could not effect my object in one way, I would resort to some other, and finally obtain it before I stopped. Indulging in this rude and mischievous disposition, I naturally became more hardened, and when at school, it was my delight to see the scholars whipped or otherwise punished, and I would often tell lies on any of them that would displease me, so as to cause them to get a flogging; and very often I would tell a lie on an innocent scholar, so as to clear a favorite and guilty one, and have the innocent one punished. It most generally happened, that I managed my villiany so as to get clear; it sometimes happened, however, that I got punished. This I did not care for any longer than the punishment lasted. So soon as I was released, I would commit a worse misdeed than the one I was chastised for, and any of my school-mates that were the cause of my punishment, I was certain to wreak my vengeance on, by having them punished in some way. From my bad conduct in school there was no teacher that would permit me to go to his school long at a time, and whenever I had any difficulty with my teachers, my mother would always protect and indulge me in what I would do; and being so indulged and protected, this excited me to commit crimes of greater magnitude. And I am frank, here to say, that my mother has been the principal and great cause of all my crimes and misfortunes, by stimulating me to the commission of those deeds that have brought me to what I am.

When I was about the age of twelve years, my mother one day sent me with a sack to a neighbor's house (Mr. Helverson's), to procure some vegetables or greens. I communicated my errand to Mrs. H., who told me to go to the garden and take what I wanted. I had no knife with me. I asked Mrs. H. to loan me a knife, which I knew she had, and she pulled out a very pretty little knife from her work-pocket, and told me not to lose or break it, for it was a present made to her by a friend. This I listened to and promised her that I would be careful. Now, while I was in the garden procuring vegetables or greens, my whole mind and wits were employed in devising some mode by which I could cheat the lady out of her knife. Finally, after I had procured my vegetables and placed them in the sack, I put the knife in the bottom of the sack; I then returned to the house, and told the lady that I laid the knife down in the garden, and had forgot the place and could not find it; I asked her to go with me and help me hunt for it, which she accordingly did, and we both hunted diligently, but to no effect. The lady was very anxious about her knife and much regretted its loss, while I was all the time laughing in my sleeve, to know how completely I had swindled her. This trick of mine passed off very well for a time. It was, however, found out that I had the knife, and that created some noise and trouble. I was accused of stealing the knife. But I denied all accusations and stated that I had bought the knife I had, in Mobile, and proved it by my mother, who always upheld me in my rascality. This may be said to have been my first successful feat in stealing, although I was in the habit of stealing little frivolous things from the school boys, before that time.

My father living a very close neighbor to Mr. Helverson, whose family is related to ours, their stock run together in the same range. My next onset in stealing was from Mr. H. again; he had a lot of very fine fat pigs, and these were at that time selling at a high price in Mobile. My brother Isham (nicknamed Whinn) and myself geared up a horse in a cart and started, pretendingly for a camp hunt to kill deer and haul to Mobile. We went a short distance that night and camped. During the night we went to Helverson's hog bed, and stole a cart load of his finest pigs, fifteen in number, hauled them to Mobile and sold them at two dollars each. Although Mr. H. was satisfied in his own mind that we had stolen his pigs, yet he could not prove it; and I escaped again. So I was stimulated with my success, and being still more encouraged and upheld by my mother, and not exceeding fourteen years of age, I believed that I could make an independent fortune by thieving, and became insensible of the danger which awaited me. A short time after the incident just related had transpired, I made a second rake upon Mr. H.'s pigs. But in my second adventure, I was not so fortunate as I was in the first, for Mr. H. *rather got me* that time. The proof was sufficiently strong, and I was prosecuted, for the first time, for pig stealing. Well knowing my guilt as I did, and the evidence against me, I thought my case extremely doubtful. I was arrested by the sheriff of Jackson county, and had to give bond to appear at the Circuit Court of Jackson county, to answer an indictment preferred against me by the State of Mississippi, for the crime of larceny. The bond required me to attend the Court from term to term, and from day to day, until discharged by due course of law. My poor old father employed the best counsel to defend me, that could be obtained in all the country. This cost the poor old man a large sum of money. My counsel, after learning the facts of the case, advised me that my only chance of acquittal, was to put off the trial as long as possible. This he did from term to term, in hopes that something might occur to get me acquitted. I well knew if my case should be brought to a hearing, I would be convicted, and I dreaded the consequences; for I knew that there would then be no chance on earth to prevent my being sent to the penitentiary.

Fully sensible of my situation, young as I was at that time, it became necessary for me to devise some plan to get out of the scrape, and I reflected for weeks how to manage this matter. One day, in a conversation with my mother and some other confidential friends, she and they advised me to consult GALE H. WAGES; and my mother said she would send for Wages and see him herself, as he was a particular friend of hers. This she accordingly did, and he came to our house. There were several of the clan at our house then, though I did not know them at that time as such; but my mother did, as I afterward found out when I joined them. Among the many plans proposed by the clan, none seemed to suit my mother or Wages. Some were for waylaying and killing the witnesses; some for one thing, and some for another. Finally Wages made his proposition, which was seconded by my mother. This was the proposition I had been waiting to hear, for my mother told me that whatever plan Wages would pursue, he would be certain to get me clear. His plan was, that we should, in some way or other, endeavor to have the Court house and all the records destroyed, and so destroy the indictment against me. By that means there would be nothing against me, and I should be acquitted, as no charge would rest against me.

With this plan I was highly pleased, and much elated with the idea that I had a friend fully able and competent to bear me out, and who would stand up to me at any and all hazards, and bring me out clear. Wages pledged himself to me in private to do this, and he was as good as his word. We set a time for the accomplishment of our design, and we accordingly met. The precise date I cannot recollect, but it was a dry time, and a dark night, with a strong breeze from the North. After procuring sufficient dry combustibles, we entered the Court-house, went up stairs, and placed our combustibles in the roof, on the windward side of the house. Wages went down-stairs to patrol around. After reconnoitering around sufficiently, he gave me the signal, by a rap or knock on the wall; I immediately sprung open the door of my darklantern, applied the match, and made my escape down stairs, and Wages and myself left the place in double quick time. We halted on an eminence some five or six hundred yards to the southeast of the Court house, to watch the conflagration. Such a sight I never had before beheld. The flames seemed to ascend as high, if not higher than the tops of the tallest pine trees; they made everything perfectly light for over two hundred yards around. After the Court house, records and all were completely consumed, and the flames had abated and died away, we took our departure for home, rejoicing at our success in the accomplishment of our design. There was a great deal of talk and conjecture about the burning of the Court house, and we were accused—at least, I was strongly censured, but there never was any discovery made, nor any proof sufficient to get hold of either Wages or myself; so I again got clear of a crime of which I was guilty and for which I ought to have been punished.

The assistance, advice and protection I had received from Wages, gave me the utmost confidence in him, and he had unbounded influence over me; I looked on him as my warmest and most confidential friend, and I eventually pinned my whole faith on him and relied upon him for advice and directions in everything. Although a villain, as I must now acknowledge Wages was, yet he had some redeeming traits in his character. At his own home he was friendly, kind and hospitable; in company, he was affable and polite; and no person at first acquaintance, would have believed for one moment, that he was the *out lawed brigand* that he finally proved himself to be; and I firmly believe he would have spilt the last drop of blood in his veins to protect me; yet I must say that he was the principal author of my misfortunes, and has brought me where I am.

After the burning of the Court House, the intercourse between Wages and myself became more frequent. We became strongly allied to each other, and confidence was fully established between us. Wages one day made a proposition to me; to join him, and go with him, alleging that we could make money without work, and live in ease and genteel style; that there were a great many persons concerned with him, in different parts of the country, some of them men of wealth and in good standing in the community in which they lived; that they had an organized *Band* that would stand up to each other at all hazard; that they had a *Wigwam* in the city of Mobile, where they held occasional meetings; and that they had many confederates there whom the public little suspected. To this proposition I readily acceded; it corresponded with my disposition and idea of things, and then, being the age I was, and stimulated by my past success, I feared nothing.

I went to Mobile with Wages, and there he introduced me to

some of his comrades, who were members of his Clan. They accordingly held a meeting at their *Wig wam*, and I was there introduced by Wages, (who was their president,) as a candidate for membership, I should have been rejected, had Wages not interceded for me. I was finally passed and admitted to membership. Wages then administered to me the oath, which every member had to take. I was then instructed and given the signs and pass-words of the Clan; and above all was cautioned to keep a watchful eye, and not to let any person entrap me; nor let any person, under pretence of belonging to the Clan, or wishing to join, obtain in any way information from me in relation to the existence of the Clan, or their plan or mode of operation. The oath was administered on the Holy Bible. (Oh! what a profanation of that good book!) The form of the oath was: "You solemnly swear upon the Holy Evangelist of Almighty God, that you will never divulge, and always conceal and never reveal any of the signs or pass-words of our order; that you will not invent any sign, token or device by which the secret mysteries of our order may be made known; that you will not in any way betray or cause to be betrayed any member of this order—the whole under pain of having your head severed from your body—so help you God."

Wages was President and Chief of the Clan. All important business of the Clan was entrusted to his care. He called meetings, gave all notices to the Clan for their gatherings, and when assembled he presided in the chair. In all matters, he had the preferred right to introduce resolutions for the benefit of the Clan.

There were present at this meeting, Charles McGrath, Vice-President; McClain, Secretary; John Eelva, Henry Sanford, Richard Cabel and Sampson Teapark, Vigilant Committee; William Brown, of Mobile, Tyler.

After I was thus initiated, and invested with all the signs, words and tokens, and fully instructed in the mysteries of the Clan, I was taught their mode of secret correspondence, by means of an alphabet or key, invented by the notorious Murrell, of Tennessee. I was furnished with the alphabet and key, and in that same mystic writing I was furnished with a list of all the names that belonged to our Clan, and a list of several other Clans, that ours was in correspondence with, their several places of residence, and the locations of their Wig-wams; so that when we stole a horse, a mule, or a negro, we knew precisely where to carry them, to have them concealed and sold.

After I had been thus fully initiated and had become identified with the Clan, Wages and McGrath, knowing my ability, and that I was a keen shrewd and cunning lad, took me under their immediate special charge. We had a rendezvous at old Wages' about twelve miles from Mobile, and another at Dog River, about the same distance in a different direction. We ranged that season from one place to the other, and sometimes in town, stealing any and everything we could. Sometimes killing beef, hogs and sheep, hauling them to town and selling them; sometimes stealing a fine horse or mule and conveying it to some of our comrades to conceal; and occasionally a negro would disappear. All this while, we pretended to be engaged in making shingles, burning charcoal, and getting laths and pickets, each for himself. We always managed to furnish the family with all the meat they could use.

We worked on in this way until late in the summer or early in the fall of 1839, when most of the inhabitants had left the city; and we having six of our Clan then employed as City Guards, we rallied our forces and Wages ordered a meeting. It was there resolved that we should prepare ourselves with boats and teams—the boats to be stationed at a particular wharf in Mobile, on a certain night, and the teams at a landing named, on Dog River the next night. It was also ordered that we should assemble at our Wig-wam on the first night at seven o'clock. The meeting then adjourned.

The promised evening came, and every member was punctual in his attendance. It was a full meeting of the Clan. We all rigged ourselves out with false moustaches, some with false whiskers, some with a green patch over one eye, and many of them dressed like sailors, and thus fitted out and disguised, we were ready for action, with all kinds of false keys, skeleton keys, lock picks, crow bars, &c. At nine o'clock the City Guards turned out, and by a previous arrangement, those of our comrades who mounted guard, were on the first watch. They immediately sent two of their number to inform us where to make the first break. They had reconnoitered previously and knew what places had the richest and most valuable goods, and they had also procured false keys for several stores. Thus armed, each man with his revolver, bowie knife and dark lantern, about ten o'clock we started out. Our first break was a fancy dry-goods store which we opened with one of our keys. We took over $5,000 worth of goods from that store, fine silks, muslins, &c. We next entered a rich jewelry store, and made a clean sweep there. There were no fine watches; we got some silver watches and two or three gold watches, left, we supposed, to be repaired. Our raise there was about four to five thousand dollars. Our next break was on a large clothing store. There we took $3000 worth of the finest and best clothing. While we were at this, some of the clan were packing off and storing in their boats. We had procured two butcher carts, which would stand a short distance off and our men packed and loaded the carts, which they hauled to our boats. About half-past eleven o'clock, knowing that there would be a new guard out at twelve o'clock. we dispersed and set fire to each of the stores we had robbed. Soon there was the cry of fire; the wind commenced blowing, and the fire spread rapidly. Our Clan now commenced operations anew; we seized and carried out goods from any and every store we came to, still retaining the carts. We kept them constantly employed; and before daylight we had loaded two large, swift boats, and had a large quantity of merchandise in a "wood flat." A little before daylight, we left with our boats for Dog River. We arrived there about eight o'clock, ten miles from the city, and went up the river to our landing place, where we secreted our goods until that night, when we had our teams at work, hauling off and concealing goods, which we finally accomplished the second night. Wages then ordered a meeting of the clan, and punctual attendance was required. The object of this meeting was for a report from each member of the amount of goods he had obtained, so that an equal distribution might be made. From the report then made, we had procured over twenty-five thousand dollars worth of goods of almost every description. We had an abundant supply of groceries and liquors. Our friends in the city had a bountiful supply of almost everything. We made a division of our plunder, and Wages, McGrath and myself got for our share about six thousand dollars worth. We were permitted to select the finest and most costly goods, such as the jewelry, fine silks, muslins etc., which we could carry in our trunks.

Having properly stowed away our effects, we took a trip from Mobile to Florida by way of Pensacola, carrying with us some of the jewelry, watches and dry goods. We traveled from Pensacola through Florida, with our pack of goods, as pedlars, each taking a different route, and all to meet at Apalachicola on a certain day. Wages went the middle route, McGrath the southern route, and I went the northern route. I traveled some distance, occasionally selling some of my plunder. I eventually arrived at a very rich neighborhood, near the Chatochooca river, not far from the Alabama line. There I soon disposed of most of my goods.

I fell in with a house where a very rich old widow lady lived. She bought a good deal of my jewelry and other goods for her two young daughters. I pretended to be sick, for an excuse to stay there. This lady had a very nice mulatto girl about seventeen years old. During the time I was there pretending to be sick, I made an arrangement with this girl to run away with me; I promised to take her for a wife, and carry her to a free State. She was to meet me on a certain night at the landing on the river, about one mile from that place. I left the house pretending to go to Columbus, Ga., and traveled up the river some thirty miles, where I stole a canoe. I procured some meat and bread and started down the river. On the night appointed I was at the landing, and about ten o'clock the mulatto girl came. She had provided bed clothing and provisions in plenty. I then started down the river with my girl. We went about thirty miles that night, and lay by in the river swamp all next day. The next night we made about fifty miles down the river. The third night we reached Apalachicola, two days previous to the time appointed to meet Wages and McGrath. I landed a short distance above town, and left my girl in a swamp just after daylight, and then went to the city. In looking around I fell in with John Harden, he being one of our clan. He soon gave me an introduction to a place where I could conceal my girl, and stay myself. The next day McGrath arrived; I met him in the street, and gave him a sign to follow me to our rendezvous. I showed him my girl and told him the way I had got her; he then told me that he had stolen a likely negro fellow, and had him concealed in a swamp about four miles from town. After dinner, and a little before night, McGrath and I went out to the swamp, brought in his fellow, and concealed him at the same place where my girl was.

The next day about eight o'clock Wages came up; we were all on the lookout for him. We gave him a hint to come to our place. We showed Wages what a raise we had made; he then told us that he had stolen two negroes and two fine horses, and that they were concealed in the swamp about five miles from town. In fear of pursuit he said we must leave instanter. We made an arrangement with Harden and our landlord to take the horses. They gave Wages twenty-five dollars a piece for the horses, and our board bill. That night

Wages and Harden went out to the swamp; Harden took the horses and left, and Wages brought in his negroes and placed them with ours. That night while Wages was gone after his negroes McGrath and I went to a coffee house, and while there we met some Spaniards that had a little schooner there, and which was then loaded for New Orleans. We made the arrangement with them to carry us and our negroes to New Orleans, returned to our place, and had everything prepared. About ten o'clock Wages came in with his negroes, and we all went on board the vessel, which weighed anchor and sailed down the bar. Next morning the captain cleared his vessel, and by ten o'clock we were over the bar and under way, with a good breeze. On the second night, a little before day, we landed at the Pontchartrain railroad, and left in the first cars for the city. We went into one of our places in the city, got breakfast for ourselves and negroes, and at nine o'clock we left in a steamboat for Bayou Sara. We landed there, crossed the river and went to one of our clan—a rich planter—where we sold our negroes. I got one thousand dollars for my mulatto girl; McGrath sold his fellow for eleven hundred dollars, and Wages sold each of his boys for nine hundred dollars. We took our money and left for Mobile. My girl made considerable fuss when I was about to leave, but I told her I would return in a month, and rather pacified her. I must here acknowledge that my conscience did that time feel mortified, after the girl had come with me, and I had lived with her as a wife, and she had such implicit confidence in me. My conscience still feels mortified when I reflect how much better it would have been for me to have kept her and lived with her than to come to what I have.

On our way to Mobile we stopped in New Orleans three or four days. During our stay there was one fire. We made a small raise on that of about one hundred dollars each. McGrath came very near being caught by attempting to make a second haul. We left next day for Mobile; landed at Pascagoula, and walked home by land, with our money and the small amount of goods we had stolen in New Orleans.

We then deposited our money, and gathered all the balance of our fine goods that we had stolen in Mobile at the great fire, and what we had stolen in New Orleans, and prepared ourselves for a second tour. We had realized about four thousand five hundred dollars, which we hid in the ground, and we took each of us about one hundred and fifty dollars for our expenses, and an equal share of the goods.

On the 25th day of March, 1843, Wages, McGrath and myself left Mobile bound to Texas; we went to New Orleans, where we landed the next day. We remained there about three days and sold a great quantity of our goods, such as were too heavy to carry. While we were in the city Wages won about seven hundred dollars from a Tennessee corn dealer by the name of Murphy. McGrath and myself had lost about one hundred and fifty dollars each. We left New Orleans, went up the Mississippi, and landed at the house of an old friend that belonged to our clan. His name was Welter. We spent one day and night with him; we had seen him in the city a few days before, and were invited to call, but when we approached his residence we all pretended to be entire strangers. This was a strict injunction upon our clan—when traveling never to meet any of our comrades as acquaintances, but always treat them as entire strangers, that we had never seen in our life.

Wages pretended to have some business with the old gentleman, and introduced himself, McGrath and myself under fictitious names. The old gentleman had two very nice genteel daughters. They were sociable and refined, well educated, and highly accomplished every way; he was wealthy, and had a good reputation in his neighborhood, and no one would for one moment have suspected him of belonging to our clan. But I afterward learned from Wages that this old gentleman had belonged to the Murrell Clan for many years; and that was what carried Wages there, to get some information relative to

C—3

some negroes that had been stolen and carried to Louisiana near the Texas line. Wages also informed me that this same man made all his property by stealing and kidnapping negroes from Kentucky, Tennessee, Virginia, Ohio, Indiana and Illinois. Having obtained the information we wanted, we made preparation to leave. We offered to pay our fare, but this was promptly refused. We were well entertained; the old gentleman furnished us each with a flask of good brandy, and, after thanking him and his family for their kind, hospitable treatment, we bid adieu, and took our departure for Texas.

We got on a steamboat and went up the Mississippi to the mouth of Red river, and up that river to a landing called the New Springs. There we paid our passage and went on shore, each with his pack and his double-barrel gun. We stopped at a house about one mile from the river, where we called for our dinner, which we got, and we all remained there until next day, during which time we sold a considerable amount of our goods at that house and in the neighborhood, which made our packs much lighter. We left next day, stopping at all houses, and selling our goods, which we did at a rapid rate, as we had stolen them and were not sufficient judges of their value to know what price to ask, and in consequence we often sold them at one-half their value, and so soon got rid of them.

Having disposed of the principal part of our goods, about the fourth day after we left the New Spring landing, we were approaching the prairie county on the Texas border. We provided ourselves with bread and salt; we had ammunition. Shortly before night, we came to a small piece of woodland, by a ravine. There was a large drove of cattle of all sizes there; McGrath shot a very fat two-year old heifer; we skinned the hind quarters and tenderloin; we built up a fire, salted some of our meat and roasted it by the fire and feasted sumptuously. The wolves came near our camp and made a dreadful noise, but at daybreak we shot and killed three and the balance ran off. They had devoured all the heifer's meat, but we had provided sufficient for our journey that day. We set out and traveled in a direction to find a settlement, then made about twenty-five miles south of Shreveport. That was the place where Welter had told Wages that the negroes were, that we were after. We traveled about thirty miles that day, and suffered very much for water. We reached a settlement a little before night, on some of the waters of the Sabine River. It was the residence of some stock keepers; there were some three or four families, and some fifteen or twenty Mexican drovers, and horse thieves; they had just been to Natchitoches, and had a full supply of rum; a few of them could speak English. We quartered with them, and that night we opened the little remnant of our goods and jewelry, and had a general raffle. By the next day we had realized from our raffle, sufficient to purchase each of us a good Spanish saddle and bridle, and a good Texas horse. We learned from one of these Mexicans the residence of the man who owned the negroes that we were after, and we also learned that he and his family were strict members of the Methodist Church. Now it was that one of us had to turn preacher, so as to reconnoiter around the place. Wages and I put that on McGrath. We all mounted our horses and started, having procured plenty of lassoes, &c., McGrath being an Irishman and his tongue tipped with plenty of blarney.

We traveled for two days very moderately, and, our chief employment was drilling McGrath, how to pray and sing, and give that long Methodist groan, and "Amen." He having made considerable progress, we went to Natchitoches. McGrath entered that town by one road, and Wages and myself by another. McGrath went among a few of his brethren that evening.

To our astonishment it was posted at every corner, that the "Rev. Mr. McGrath, from Charleston, South Carolina, would preach at the Methodist Church that evening, at half-past seven." We attended church. McGrath took his stand in the pulpit. He made a very genteel apology to his audience, saying he was much fatigued from his travel; that he had caught cold and was very hoarse and could not sing; but he read out the hymn. It was: "Hark from the tombs a doleful sound," One old brother pitched the tune to Old Hundred, and they all chimed in, Wages and myself among the rest; Wages sang bass and I tenor, and we all made that old church sound like distant thunder. After singing, McGrath made a very good but short prayer; he then took his text in the 16th chapter of St. Mark, at the verse where Mary the mother, and Mary Magdalene found the stone rolled from the door of the sepulchre. "And he said unto them, Be not affrighted; ye seek Jesus of Nazareth, who was crucified; he has risen; he is not here; behold the place where they laid him." He read several verses in that chapter, and then made some very good explanations relative to the parables, and prophesies on the coming of the Messiah, and the mysterious way in which he disappeared, and wound up his discourse by telling the audience that he had been a great sinner in his young days, that it had been but a few years since the Lord had called him to preach, and he thanked his God that he was now able and willing to lay down his life upon the altar of God; he then raved, and exhorted all to repent and turn to God; and after raving about half an hour called all his hearers that wished to be prayed for to come forward. The whole congregation knelt down; he prayed for them all, and finally finished, sang another hymn and dismissed his congregation, and we all retired, Wages and myself to a gaming table, and McGrath with some of his brethren. Next day the members of the church there waited on McGrath to know what was his pecuniary situation. He told them that he was very poor, was on his way to see a rich relation of his, about two hundred miles from there; that he carried his gun to keep off wild beasts, etc. They made up money to buy him a fine suit of black, a new saddle and saddle-bags and fifty dollars in cash. We remained there two days, when McGrath left. Wages and I left by another road. We all met a short distance from town and made the proper arrangement for our operations. McGrath was to go on to the house of this man that had the negroes, and there make what discoveries were necessary. He was to join Wages and myself at San Antonio on the first day of September following. Wages and I left in the direction for the Red Land on the Irish bayou.

### POISONING THE OVERSEER.

A few days after we passed the residence of an old bachelor who had a large number of negroes; he was absent at Natchitoches and had left his overseer in charge. We stopped there, and remained two days; we procured some whisky from a grocery store a short distance off; prepared some of it with *poison*, and induced the overseer to drink freely. We gave him a full dose of the poison, and before day on the third morning he was dead.

Meanwhile Wages and I had made arrangements to steal a likely negro woman and two young negroes, a boy and girl, about ten years of age, besides two of the finest horses on the place. We sent out runners to let one or two of the neighbors know that the overseer was dead; we had our negroes and horses concealed about five miles distant, and about sunrise we offered to pay our bills and left, pretending to go to New Orleans. After we had got out of sight of the plantation we made a circuit and went to the place where the negroes and horses were concealed. Having provided ourselves with provisions, we remained secreted at that place all that day. That night we started with our negroes and horses. Wages took the lead; our horses and negroes were all refreshed. We traveled a brisk gait all that night and till next day at nine or ten o'clock. We suffered greatly for water, having met with none after midnight, until we stopped at a small creek. We had passed no houses after daylight. After we stopped we stripped our horses, gave them water and hampered them to graze; we got water for ourselves and negroes, and took a little spirits we had, and eat the balance of our provisions. After we had rested a little while, Wages took his gun and went up the creek in search of game; I took mine and went to the road we had just left, and went on rather down the creek. At the distance of about two miles I came to a plantation. It was an old stock place, inhabited by some of the old creole settlers that had lived there in Spanish times. I inquired the distances and courses of the country. They told me it was about forty miles to the first river, and that there was but one settlement on the road where we could get water for ourselves and horses, at about twenty-five miles. After I had got this information I purchased some bread and potatoes and a small piece of dried beef, and returned to our camp. Wages had killed a fine deer, and he and the negro woman were roasting a fine piece. We fared well that day. That night about dark we left our camp, provided with provisions for two days. A little after midnight we reached the first water. A little before daylight we reached some settlements and woodland; we traveled a short distance and came to a small, deep river. We there found a ferry flat and some small boats. We took the flat and carried our horses and negroes over; took the flat back, and took a small boat, and Wages and I crossed to our horses and negroes. By this time we could discern the appearance of day. We mounted and traveled on; we could perceive we were passing several large plantations; by sunrise we had traveled four or five miles. We could see at a distance several clusters of woodland in the prairies. We made for one of them some distance from the road, which we found afforded sufficient shelter for that day. We found some water, but not plenty, and very bad; our horses would drink but little of it. We stripped and hampered our horses to graze, took our breakfast and told the negroes to go to sleep. I went to sleep, and Wages kept watch. About twelve o'clock I was awakened by the report of a gun. I rose up and found that Wages had shot a fat yearling beef. We skinned and saved the hind quarters and loin, and salted it a little and barbecued it. While Wages lay down and took a nap the negro woman and I attended to the meat. About an hour before sunset Wages awoke, and we all eat heartily. We eat the last of our bread and potatoes; our horses had finished grazing and were resting, and about sunset we began to pack up for traveling, with plenty of meat and no bread. About dark we left our sheltered woods and started on the road again. We were then about one hundred and twenty miles from the place where we had stolen the negroes. We traveled on that night about thirty miles, and reached a large creek between midnight and day. We passed one or two plantations, and very little woodland. When Wages came to the creek he examined the ford and found horse tracks; he rode in first, went over and came back, and took the bridle of the horse that had the two little negroes and led him safely across, and the negro woman and myself followed. We went on some seven or eight miles, and came to woodland and plantations again. Some of the plantations were very large. We continued traveling till daylight; after day we passed several fine, large plantations. The sun was about one hour high when we came to a ferry on a large river. We called, and the ferryman was a negro; we inquired the distance from the last river we had crossed; he said sixty-three miles. The negro was a very intelligent fellow; we inquired particularly for San Antonio, and told him there was where we were going. We inquired for several other places, and left; at a short distance we found a place where we could rest, not far from a plantation. There Wages and myself procured some corn for our horses, the first they had eaten for several days. We also procured some bread; after we had fed and rested our horses and slept some ourselves, a little before night we started again. We traveled that night about thirty-five miles, and stopped at a small creek and camped till daylight. We then started, crossed the creek, went out a short distance and turned our course more to the east. We took a trail that led us down the creek.

We halted about noon to rest our horses, which by this time were much fatigued. Here we procured something for ourselves to eat.

We were now over two hundred miles from the place where we had stolen the negroes; we here enquired for several places and where was the best place to locate. We wanted to find a rich neighborhood where there was good society, etc. We got directions for several places, among the rest the lower settlement on the Brasos river. After we had rested, late in the afternoon, we set out, pretending to be bound for San Antonio, but we steered our course for the Brasos river, where we arrived the second day after. We quartered our negroes with a planter there and traveled around. We at length found a purchaser, some twenty miles from the place where the negroes were. We delivered them to him and received the pay for them—sixteen hundred dollars. We took the horses about forty miles and sold one, and about thirty miles further we sold the other. We then went some distance and sold our own horses.

We had realized from all our sales a little short of two thousand dollars. This was about the tenth of May. The money was principally in New Orleans Bank bills, and we had some gold and silver to pay our little expenses. We now steered our course for San Antonio, on foot, and reached there in about five days. We traveled leisurely, and procured some two-headed Texas gourds to carry our water through the prairies. After resting a day or two, we looked around to see how the land lay. We went into a store and bought two light Spanish saddles, with bridles and all the apparatus for riding. We put them up in a genteel package, and provided ourselves with provisions for two days. Each shouldered his pack, and we left San Antonio in the night, and steered our course west. We had traveled some ten or fifteen miles, when we stopped at a small creek and camped. Next morning we traveled on some twenty-five miles farther, when we came to a ranche, where there was a great stock of horses, mules, jacks, jennies and horned cattle. We hid our saddles before we approrched the place, and went up with our bundles of clothes and guns and asked for something to eat, which was given us—plenty milk and bread. Only one or two of the people could speak English, and that very indifferently. An old man, the head of the place, and his drover and herdsman, spoke the best English. We asked the old man to let us have a couple of horses and saddles, and we would go with him a hunting and take our guns; we told him we wished to see the country; he told us "yes," and furnished us with horses. We spent a week or more with him. We killed plenty of venison to supply the whole ranche.

### MURDER OF THE TWO MEXICANS IN TEXAS.

One day Wages told him that we wanted to go and camp out that night about twenty-five miles off; we would be back next night, and wanted one of his gentle mules to pack; he told us to take the mule and any horses we pleased, and helped us to pack up, with water, provisions and whatever we wanted. We started and remained out that night and the next, and returned the third day. We had seven fine deer in all; he asked what kept us so long—had we been lost? We told him we had, and that while we were out we had met with an acquaintance of ours, buying horses and mules, and that he had furnished us money to buy thirty good horses and thirty mules, if we could get them delivered at a certain place named, about one hundred miles from there. We showed him the gold we had, and satisfied him as to the money, which was to be paid on delivery of the horses and mules at the place mentioned. The horses and mules were selected, and the price agreed upon. Gentle lead and pack mules were selected, and every preparation was made for our departure. We were to go with him and return with him, so as to see that the contract was complied with. The day arrived and we set out with five mules packed, and five gentle lead mules, with bells on, and a young half-breed Indian to assist in driving, and all of us mounted on the best of horses. We had managed to procure our new saddles and put them in their packs, on a mule that was set apart for us. Thus equipped, with plenty of water and provisions, we set out a little after daylight. Our travel that day was upwards of thirty miles, on account of having water. The next day was farther. We however made the two points. The next day our only stopping place was about twenty miles, and the next was thirty miles.

This twenty-mile place appeared to be a dead lake or spring, with an underground discharge, with a few small groves of timber near by, and several lakes or sinks in the ground, in the direction the water was supposed to run under ground. We left our second night's camp on the third morning, and arrived at the twenty-mile place in the forenoon. We, as usual, stripped and hampered our horses to graze, eat dinner, and the old Mexican and his man lay down to sleep. Wages and I took our guns and went off, pretending to hunt. We killed a turkey and a prairie hen and a small deer. We cleaned our guns, wiped them out, loaded them with the largest buck-shot, took our game and went to the camp. While loading our guns, we made the arrangement in what way to dispatch our traveling companions, for that was the way we intended to pay for the horses and mules. So it was agreed that the next morning, before day, we were to prepare some dry gass and have our guns ready; Wages was to get up, wake me, and we were to set the straw on fire, to make a light to see the position in which the two men lay.

All that night I did not sleep one minute of sound sleep. The most awful and frightful dreams infested my mind all night, and Wages told me the next day that his sleep was disturbed in the same way, and he then regretted the act and wished he had not done it.

Wages rose in the morning and easily waked me, for I was not in a sound sleep. We took our guns; I crawled close to where the young man lay, and got my gun ready. Wages was to fire first. He put his light against a small brush, and the old man partly waked and turned his face toward Wages, who fired the contents of one barrel in the old man's forehead.

The young man was lying with his back to me; I placed the muzzle of my gun to the back of his head, where the neck joined it. My finger was on the trigger. At the report of Wages' gun, I pulled the trigger, and there was but little distinction in the report of the two guns.

Both men gave a suppressed, struggling scream, and expired.

Our next work was to dispose of them, which we did by slinging them with ropes, swinging them on a pole, carrying them to one of the sink holes close to the camp, and burying them there. We deposited with them all the clothes that had any blood on them; and with the hatchet they had, we sharpened a short pole and partially covered them with dirt. We next went to the camp and raked out with sticks and brush all the signs of blood, and took brush and dry leaves and built fires on the ground where we had killed them. All of this we had accomplished by a little before sunrise.

Our next work was to prepare to leave the place. We took the old man's fine massive silver spurs, his silver stirrups and silver bridle bits, his gold rings, sleeve buttons, etc. We took our new saddle and bridles, and concealed all the old ones in the prairie, about five miles from the camp. After we had arranged everything to our liking, we gathered our pack mules and packed them; herded up the lead mule and the drove; Wages mounted the old man's horse, and I the young man's, we tied our other two horses together and turned them in the drove, and all things being now completed, we set out about eight o'clock in the morning.

We now had the sixty horses and mules and the ten lead and pack mules, the two fine horses of the old man and his servant, and the two horses he had loaned us to ride, which made seventy-four head in all, and a better selected drove of horses never left Texas. We pursued our journey that day very silent. Wages had but little to say and I had less. We had in our hurry and confusion forgotten to supply ourselves with water, and had but little victuals to eat that were cooked. About a quart of water in our gourds, was all we had for the day. We came to the water late in the evening. We suffered very much for water that day, as did our horses. We stripped and hampered them to graze, after they had got water, and then prepared some thing for ourselves. We had our turkey and part of the deer; we built a fire and barbecued the game. After we had eat, Wages said he could not sleep, and told me to lie down and take a nap.

I laid down, but could not sleep. Every time I would fall into a doze, the vision of the young man I had killed the night before, would appear before my eyes, and I would start up in a fright. After several ineffectual attempts, I finally got up, and told Wages I could not sleep, and told him to try it. He laid down and was quite still for some time. All at once he screamed out "Oh! my God!" and jumped upon his feet. I called and asked what was the matter, and he declared that he saw the old man he had killed, standing over him, and that he plainly saw the shot holes in his head, and the blood running down his face. So we both set up the balance of the night.

The next morning we started very early. About noon we came to a large creek where we procured plenty of water for ourselves and the drove; we halted and rested awhile, and then pursued our journey with little delay, making the route as direct as possible for the mouth of Red River. We did not pass the settlement on Irish Bayou, nor Natchitoches. We arrived at the mouth of Red River and went down the river until we came opposite Bayou Sara, where we had our horses and mules ferried over.

We went to a man living out from the river, and effected a

sale of all the horses, except the four saddle horses. We went up into Wilkinson County, Mississippi, where we sold all the mules, getting fifty dollars for each of the horses and an average of seventy-five dollars for each of the mules. We sold the two saddle horses that Wages and myself rode before we killed the two Mexicans, for one hundred dollars each. We then shaped our course for Natchez, and when within about twenty miles of it, we effected sale of the two horses we were riding, to one man; he gave Wages one hundred and fifty dollars for the horse the old Mexican had, and he gave me one hundred and twenty-five dollars for the one I rode, and sent us in a carriage to Natchez, where we arrived about the last of June. We had realized on our trip that time about six thousand six hundred and seventy-five dollars.

We had not been in Natchez long before a steamboat passed down and we went on board. We had preserved our saddles, bridles and all our traveling equipage. We landed at New Orleans, went to the bank and deposited all our money, but a few hundred dollars, which we retained in gold coin—two and a half and five dollar pieces. We remained in New Orleans to spend the fourth of July with our associates there.

On the 5th of July, 1841, Wages and I left New Orleans and embarked on a small steamboat bound to Shreveport on Red River, taking with us our saddles, bridles and traveling equipage. In consequence of very dry weather Red River was very low. We had some delay in getting to Shreveport. We, however, reached there, and found some wagons traveling out to the interior of Texas. We made arrangements with them to haul our baggage, and we traveled with them part of the time, some times before them and some times behind. We kept with us our bridles and ropes or lassoes. About the fourth day after we left Shreveport, we started on before the wagons, and traveled some fifteen to twenty miles. By noon we came to a settlement on the border of a small river, one branch of the Trinity, we supposed, and there rested and eat some bread and meat. In the evening we reconnoitered and discovered in the vicinity a large, newly settled plantation, a good number of horses and mules grazing around, and a large number of negroes about the place. Wages sent me to watch on the main road for the wagons, while he watched the horses and mules. About sunset a negro came to drive the horses and mules to their lot. Wages asked what his master's name was and what State he moved from. He told Wages his master's name was Smith; and he moved from South Carolina. Wages asked if he was a good master. The negro said no; that he did not feed well nor clothe well, and that he drove hard and whipped hard. Wages then told the negro, if he would come down that night to the ferry, which was about two miles off, he would give him a shirt and pantaloons and a dram. Wages then came to where I was stationed on the road, but the wagons had passed about one hour before. We hurried on and got to the ferry a little after dark. The wagons had just got over and were camped on the other bank. We called, and the ferryman let us over, and went to his house some distance off. We took supper with the wagons. After supper, Wages and I feigned an excuse to cross the river to bathe. We took with us a flask of whiskey and the shirt and pantaloons Wages had promised the negro, and crossed in the ferry flat. We made fast the flat, went up the bank and there we found the negro, true to his promise. Wages gave him the dram and the shirt and pantaloons. Wages then asked the negro if he did not want to leave his master and go to a free State. The negro said he did; that he had runaway three times in South Carolina and started to Ohio, but was caught every time. Wages then gave him another dram and asked him if he could steal three of the best horses on his master's plantation, and bring them to that ferry the next night or the night after. The negro said he could. Wages then told him, if he would bring the three horses and one bridle and saddle and go with us, that he would take him to a free State. The negro promised to do so, and said he could do it next night as well as any other time, and said he had two halters to lead with, and an old wagon saddle. We told him we had saddles and bridles. We gave him another dram and let him go, and we wet our heads and crossed over to the camp.

Next morning we told the wagoners that we would stop a few days in the vicinity, and rest awhile and hunt. We went on two or three miles, to the border of the prairie, and took out our baggage, among which we had two small three-gallon kegs of whiskey, one full, and the other with about one gallon in. We paid for hauling our things, bid the wagoners adieu, and they drove on. We shouldered our baggage, as much as we could carry; went a short distance from the road and concealed it; and went back and took the rest to the same place. We then took our flasks full of whiskey, our two gourds full of water, and some salt, and went about a mile on the edge of the prairie, where we built a small fire. We next turned out to hunt meat. We could find plenty of cattle, but were afraid to shoot them so near the settlement, for fear of discovery before we had accomplished our purpose. We hunted some time and finally came in view of a small grove of trees, about a half mile distant. Wages and I separated; I went on one side and he on the other of the grove, and we found a few deer there. We killed one small buck, which we took back to our camp and skinned and barbecued him, and eat, and prepared the rest to take with us. We laid down for a nap and awoke about an hour by sun; and took our things to where we had the others concealed. About sunset we eat our supper, took our bridles, lassoes, guns, and flasks of whiskey, and started back to the ferry, which we reached about half an hour after dark. We concealed ourselves near the landing, until about nine o'clock. Wages then took the ferry flat and went over the river; I remained on the same side to watch. If we discovered any person we were to make the noise of the swamp owl.

Wages had been across about an hour when up came the

negro, with the three horses; Wages immediatly took the negro and horses in the flat and crossed over. We soon put bridles on the horses and Wages mounted one and I mounted the other—bare backed. Wages took the lead, the negro next; and I in behind; we both had our guns well loaded and both cocked, for fear the negro had betrayed us, and we were determined to kill with every load in our guns, if attacked. We soon arrived at the place of our baggage. Wages and I very soon saddled our horses and divided our baggage and gave a part to the negro. We then divided the whiskey and had about one gallon and a half in each keg; I took one and the negro one, and we tied them to our saddles with the ropes. We filled our two flasks; Wages took our meat, and about eleven o'clock that night we all set out, Wages ahead, the negro next and I in the rear, and I assure you we pushed from the word go, all that night, mostly through prairies.

Some time before day we came to a settlement, and a little farther on we came to a small river. Knowing it must be very low, we determined to ford or swim. We started in; it was very deep. About the middle, we came to a gravelly bar. Wages halted, and said to us that he could see a ferry flat; he believed the water was very deep near the shore, and we must swim and try and land above the ferry flat. He told me to take care of my gun and ammunition and to wait until he and the negro got through and out. They started, and got to the bank. Such splashing you never did hear. Wages got out; the negro's horse bogged; he jumped off and took the bridle, and the horse got out. Wages then told me to bear up, which I did, and got through. We then got water, filled our gourds and took each a dram, mounted our horses and pushed on again till daylight appeared.

Wages and I then consulted, whether to keep on or lay by through the day. We concluded it was safer to stop, conceal the negro and horses, and watch the road. We began to look out for some woodland, and about half an hour after sunrise we descried woodland to the west, at some distance. We made for it, stripped our horses and hampered them to graze; took our dram, some water, and eat our breakfast on venison without bread, and Wages took his gun and went to watch the road, I took my gun and went west to hunt water. We left the negro to mind the horses; we took our flasks; each went his own way. I walked about a mile and came to some prairie land, and a short distance further I saw woodland and plenty of cattle and horses; I knew there must be water there. I hunted and found plenty, but it was very bad. In searching around, I found a flock of turkeys and killed two and cleaned and washed them there and went back to the camp. The negro had been tasting the contents of his keg, as he said, to make it lighter, and he was pretty tight; I told him he must stop that until we got further off; he said he would. We made a fire and roasted our turkeys. I told the negro to go to sleep, which he did. After he had slept his nap out, I laid down and told him to watch and wake me about two hours before sunset. We then put saddles on two horses and led one, and went with our gourds to the water. Our horses drank *some*; the negro drank powerfully—the whiskey he had taken down made his coppers a little hot. We filled the gourds and returned to camp, where we had dried all the traveling equipage, and we then packed and arranged everything, ready to travel when Wages should return.

About sunset he came in and informed us that no person had passed the road in pursuit of us; but that two men had passed the other way, and if we had kept on that day we should in all probability have got ourselves in trouble, for these men said they were in pursuit of two thieves who had stolen two horses and three negroes on the Irish Bayou, in April last, and that the same thieves were suspected of having poisoned the overseer on the same plantation. They told Wages they had traveled nearly all Texas; they had been to San Antonio, and all western Texas, and could get no news of the fellows. Wages then told them that he had a family and resided about twenty miles from that place, on the next river they would come to, about ten miles below the ferry; he was looking for his horses; that he had removed from South Carolina; that he crossed the Mississippi river about the first of May, and had met two men with two very good horses and three negroes, and they were near the river. He described the horses and negroes, and they declared they were the same that had been stolen. Wages then inquired if they had seen his horses. They said they had not. He then said to them: "Gentlemen, I have a little whiskey in my flask; will you take some?" They replied they would, if it did not disfurnish him. He told them he should return to a camp he had, about five miles off, where he had some comrades helping him to hunt his horses, and they had a little more there in a small jug. They drank. Wages then inquired of them about the country south and west of there, and about the roads and the water, etc. They told him it was fifteen miles to the first water—a large creek, but fordable; and that it was twenty-five miles to the next, and that was to ferry. Wages having obtained the information he required, offered them his flask again. The sun then was about one hour and a half high. He saw three men come riding from the same way we had come; they were riding very fast; they rode up and inquired which way we were traveling. Wages told them he lived east of that about twenty miles; was hunting his horse. The other two men stated they were on the hunt of some stolen horses and negroes, that were taken from the settlement on Irish Bayou, in April; that they had been through western Texas, and were now direct from San Antonio. The three men enquired how far they had traveled that day. They said from the last ferry, about forty miles. They then inquired if the two men had met any person on the road. They replied no. One of the three then said that some person had stolen a negro and three horses from them the night before, and they were in pursuit of them, and they had seen signs where they had swam the river, ten miles back. Wages then told them that just after daylight that morning his dog had awakened him, and he looked some distance off and saw a white man and a negro on horseback, traveling a new road, in a southeast direction, and about twenty miles southeast from that place. The negro had a lead horse. Then Wages described to them the horses (which were the same we had). They said they were the same, and immediately turned their course. Wages gave them some directions and they all left. Wages then hurried to our camp as fast as he possibly could.

On his arrival I could see that something was wrong; that he was irritated, and, I thought, alarmed. He was much exhausted for want of water; he took a little and a dram, eat a few mouthfuls of turkey and sat down. He told the negro to catch the horses, put the bridles on and hitch them, saddle his own horse, and have everything ready as quick as possible. The negro started. Wages then said to me: "James, I am more alarmed now than I ever have been since you and I first started out in Alabama. Our situation is truly a critical and dangerous one, and I am at a loss what to do." He then told me what information he had that day received, and then asked me what I thought it best to do. I reflected for a few moments, and this idea immediately occurred to me, and I said to Wages: "We must cross that forty-mile ferry before daylight to-morrow morning." Wages studied a few moments and said "agreed!" and we were not long in saddling up and packing all things, ready to travel. We filled our flasks with whiskey, gave our negro a good horn, and drilled him as to the mode of travel. About dark we left our place of concealment.

Wages took the lead, the negro about thirty-five yards behind, and I about thirty-five yards behind him, so as to evade any sudden surprise. We soon reached the main road, and Wages pushed on at a fast gait. In about three hours we reached the fifteen-mile creek; here we stopped about three-quarters of an hour, let our horses drink and blow; we go water, eat some of our turkey, took a dram, and gave the negro one, filled our gourds with water, and about eleven o'clock we started again, Wages in the lead, and traveled until about three o'clock in the morning. We saw a light near the road; Wages stopped and came back to me to know if he should ride up and inquire how far it was to the ferry. I told him no; that the best way would be to go round the fire and push on, which we did, and about two or three miles further we came to woodland and a plantation. We quickened our pace, and about one mile further, a little before four o'clock, we reached the ferry. Wages told me to strip off my clothes and he would do the same. We stripped, and placed the negro in the bushes with the horses. We swam over and were not many minutes getting the flat over. We put on our clothes, took the horses and negro, and crossed over. Our horses drank, and the negro filled our gourds while we were crossing. We landed, made the flat fast, as we had found it, mounted the horses and left in a hurry.

As we got out from the river we could see the appearance of day. Our horses we could discover were getting very much fagged. There was a farm at the ferry, and so we went out through a lane. We did not travel far before day, and we soon reached the outskirts of the woodland and came again to the open prairie. Wages then stopped and said we had better leave the road and lay-by again. We left the road, and went in a westerly direction, up the river, on the border of the woodland and prairie, about two miles, and then stopped. We stripped our horses and hampered them, as usual, to graze. Wages complained of being sick; was low spirited; I told him and the negro to lie down and take a nap. They eat some of my turkey, laid down, and soon went to sleep. I took a good dram and eat as much turkey as I wanted, and there was but little left. I then took my gun and hunted around a short distance; I found we were not more than one mile from a plantation; I saw plenty of stock, hogs and cattle, but was afraid to shoot one so early in the day; I hunted around for water, and above the plantation I came to the river, about one mile and a half from where our horses were. I went back to the camp; Wages and the negro were still asleep; the horses had filled themselves and were lying down under the shade of a tree. I took another dram, a little water and laid down to rest. In about an hour Wages awoke and got up; said he felt better. I then related to him my discovery; he said we must be very cautious, and told me to lie down and take a nap. I showed him the direction where the water was, and he rode one of the horses at a time, until he gave them all water; he then took the negro and they went and killed a small beef, and about sunset brought in the hind quarters. We soon had a fire of wood that did not make much smoke; roasted as much beef as we could eat; cut up the balance and dried it; took with us what we could conveniently carry, and about dark set out again, not knowing where we would get the next water. Our salt, too, had given out.

We traveled that night about twenty miles before we came to water, and that was a small creek that scarcely run, and had very little timber land about it. Wages said our safest course would be to conceal ourselves there until he could reconnoitre. We remained there until near daylight, gave our horses water and started. We soon struck the prairie, and again turned to the west and went some two miles along a trail to a piece of woodland, where we again stripped our horses and hampered them to graze. We built a fire and barbecued our meat. Wages then told me and the negro to lie down and sleep, and he would take a look around. I went to sleep, and about twelve or one o'clock Wages awoke me, and when I opened my eyes there was another man with him—a large, dark-skinned, coarse-looking fellow. Wages introduced me to Mr. James; Wages had known Ben James for many years. James then told me that he was settled there for the same business we were in, and that we would be safer with him than by going on; by remaining with him we could rest and refresh ourselves and horses, and that he would go with us to another of our clan, about one hundred miles from San Antonio, where our negro and horses would be safe until we left again for the Mississippi river. This other man's name was Scott, from Mississippi. James advised us not to sell the negro or horses in Texas; that there were plenty of men in Texas who followed hunting and trailing theives and robbers, and that they had dogs of the bloodhound breed that would be certain to overtake us if they got after us.

We went to James' place; concealed our horses and negro, and remained with him five days, during which time Wages and I watched the road closely to see if any person passed in pursuit of us, particularly at the ford of the creek.

James provided his family with meat and bread for the two weeks trip he intended to make with us. He advised us to leave the main road and go with him to the house of the man Scott. He piloted us through. We traveled the most of the way by night, and arrived at Scott's the fourth night. After making the proper arrangement with Scott, we sent our horses out in the mountains and the negro to take care of them, with a man that Scott had employed for that purpose, for we understood afterward from James that they always had from one to two hundred head of stolen horses there, which it was the business of this man James to steal and drive and sell. We paid him fifty dollars for piloting us through.

After we had rested and all things were arranged, Wages and I took our bridles and lassoes, with a few clothes in a small bundle, and left in a direction for San Antonio. It was now about the first of August. We traveled about twenty miles the first day; the weather was very hot, water was scarce, and we suffered a great deal. We changed our course so as to pass through a section of country where water was more plentiful, and on the evening of the second day we reached a settlement where there was plenty of water and the inhabitants were thickly settled. At the house of a very respectable farmer we stopped and inquired if we could rest two or three days, and were told we could. A great many questions were asked us about our journey, where we were from, where we were going, and the object of our journey; to which we answered them we were South Carolina planters looking for good land; that we were large slave holders, etc., and that we came in summer and took it on foot leisurely to ascertain the health of the country. We inquired if there were any churches in the vicinity, and were told there were none, but that traveling preachers sometimes preached at private houses. We were then informed that there was to be a large camp meeting about the middle of August about twenty miles from there. We at once agreed to attend, because we were almost certain we should meet McGrath there.

We accordingly attended, and sure enough we met that reverend gentleman. Through some of the brethren we obtained an introduction to the Rev. Mr. McGrath, and after the preliminary conversation we became very strict members of the church. We obtained a short private interview with McGrath, and made an appointment for a private conference that night; and accordingly that night, after supper, preaching and prayer meeting were over and the patrol was out and stationed, and all things were still, McGrath, Wages and I went outside of the patrol lines to hold private prayer. No one suspected anything. After we were alone McGrath inquired what success we had met with, and we related to him all we had done, in a condensed form, which seemed to astonish him when we told him we had a negro and three fine horses yet concealed and not disposed of. We then inquired his success. He had made a raise out of the religious brethren of about one thousand dollars, by begging, and they had paid for four fine horses for him, which was equivalent to about five hundred dollars more. He would sell his horse, saddle and bridle, and go to his congregation and tell them he had been robbed of his horse and all his money and clothes. The people would throw into the "hat," and buy another horse, and fit him out with new clothes and money. The horse he then had was given him about fifty miles from there, and if we would steal his horse and hide him the brethren would soon give him another. Wages did this the next night, and concealed the horse in the woods not far from a plantation, where he procured green corn to feed him, about five miles from the camp ground. Next day there was found a piece of broken rope to the tree, and the preacher's horse was gone. There was a great noise about it. McGrath told the brethren he thought he knew the place the horse would go to, and that he could obtain him if he had another horse. They furnished him with one, which he was to return if he obtained his own. The one furnished was a splendid young horse. Wages, about an hour before sunset, would stroll off and go to where the horse was, and water and feed him about dark, and back to supper and then to prayer.

The meeting lasted four days. The night before the meeting broke up, there was another preacher's horse that went the same way. He was a remarkable fine horse, and belonged to an old preacher who lived about seventy miles from the camp ground. We now had ourselves again on horseback. It was then understood between Wages, McGrath and myself that it would not be safe for us to go to San Antonio, and that we had better leave Texas as soon as possible. We arranged with McGrath to meet us at Scott's in three days. Wages and I called on some of the preachers to pray for us, announcing to them our departure on our exploring expedition on foot. Many of the brothers and sisters joined in this prayer. After receiving the benedictions of the elders of the church, Wages and I left about three o'clock. We had left our guns at a house about two miles distant from the camp ground. We took them, procured some bread and meat, and a bottle to carry some water, and then went to the place where Wages had concealed the horses, found them safe, and more green corn around them than they could have eaten in two days. We then took out our bridles from our bundles and fitted them on. Wages had stolen blankets with the horses, and two bed quilts. We arranged these to ride on, and with our ropes or lassoes, we made substitutes for stirrups. By this time it was sundown. We took our guns and looked around to see if there were any spies out. We saw no one except the people on the farm, driving in their stock. We returned to the horses, and about dark set out. Wages took the lead on McGrath's horse, a fine traveler, and I, on the other, just walked right up to him. We traveled about six miles an hour and did not push. Before day sometime, we had traveled some forty-five miles to a creek, and knew we were within twenty or twenty-five miles of Scott's. We laid by all next day. About sundown, we again started, and reached Scott's before that night.

Long before daylight next morning, our horses were sent off to the mountains with the others. The next day up rolled the Rev. Mr. McGrath. We introduced him as the Rev. Mr. McGrath, whom we had seen in South Carolina. Mr. Scott and family invited him to spend two or three days, during which time Wages, McGrath and I had a full consultation.

Having been with Wages so long, I knew his judgment to be superior to mine, and I knew that McGrath was wanting in stability; that he was too wild and uncertain in his actions; I therefore proposed to let Wages plan out our future course, which McGrath agreed to. Wages then said: "Boys, it is time some of us were leaving Texas—particularly James and I. Mac, you can remain here as a striker for us, until we get those negroes you have described to us. You say there are seven of them—two men and their wives, one of them with one and the other with two children, and the youngest child is about four years old. They will have to be carried away by water. We never can get them away by land, and the Christmas holidays will be the only time that we can effect that with safety."

"Now," said Wages, "my plan is this: You leave here before

we do, one or two days, and wait for us at some point and pilot us through to Red river, above Shreveport, where we can cross with our negro and horses and land in the Indian Nation. You can then remain and preach around until Christmas; you appoint a two or three days' meeting for the negroes near Red River; pretend to prevent frolic and drunkenness, and about that time James and I will be on hand, with a boat to effect our object; and it will be policy," said Wages to McGrath, "for you to remain some weeks after we are off with the negroes, and meet us at Natchez or Vicksburg."

McGrath agreed to this; directed us what route to take; promised that he would meet us at a river, about sixty miles from Scott's, on the fifth night from that time, and that he would wait there for us. On the morning of the fourth day McGrath bid farewell to Mr. Scott and family, promising to call and see them again, God willing. We remained two days longer; prepared ourselves with some packs and provisions, and went to the mountains where our horses were. We paid Scott fifty dollars for his trouble. We packed our horses and led them; Scott sent a pilot with us, to conduct us through the mountains, a by-way, about forty miles, which we traveled in two days; he then put us in the road to go to where we were to meet McGrath, and we met him on the night appointed. He had all things in readiness. We crossed the river and laid by in daytime and traveled by night, McGrath with us.

He would go ahead to houses, lay by and sleep, and pray for the people; and tell them that he traveled of a night from choice, on account of the heat. On the third morning after McGrath joined us, we arrived at a good place, where there was plenty of water, about thirty-five miles from Red river. There we told McGrath to ride on ahead, get his horse fed, and breakfast, and then go on to the ferry. This he did; he crossed over and stopped near the landing. The ferryman was a negro; McGrath procured a bittle of whiskey, to which he had added plenty of opium, and treated the ferryman liberally. He tied his horse up, got corn from the ferryman, and by eleven o'clock he had the ferryman as limber as a cotton rag. He then took the ferry flat and crossed over to meet us. We got to the ferry about two o'clock, crossed over and traveled until daylight, McGrath with us. After day we turned off from the road to a place where some Indian families lived, and there bought some corn, meat and bread, and fed our horses and ourselves, and rested that day, and started again that night, McGrath with us. That night we traveled about forty miles; next morning we traveled until we found a place off the main road where we could rest secure. Here we stopped again with Indians. We procured plenty for ourselves and horses, and rested that day. Here we made our arrangements permanent, and reduced them to black and white, in our usual mystic character. We were to meet above Shreveport a few miles, on the 20th of December coming, with a proper skiff, prepared with provisions, etc.

All matters thus arranged, McGrath took off his traveling hunting shirt and straw hat; put on his long, straight-breasted bombazine coat and his broad-brimmed black beaver, and gave us a sound of his colloquial benediction of, "Hark from the tombs, gentlemen," and steered his course southeast, into Louisiana towards Alexandria; whilst we steered our course to the northeast in the direction for the Washita below Monroe, some fifty miles.

We soon got into the settlements and began to feed and rub our horses and blanket them. It was now September; cotton was to pick out, plenty; we pursuaded our negro he had better pick out cotton a while, until we could sell the horses and get money to carry us to Cincinnati; he agreed. We cautioned him about answering questions, which he had his instructions how to answer. We hired him to a man in an obscure place on Black River or Bayou; we traveled out through the country and soon sold our fine horses and for a fine price. We got from one hundred and seventy-five to two hundred and thirty dollars apiece. We sold all the horses before the first of October; they averaged us a little short of a thousand dollars. While selling, we met with a man by the name of Harden; he said he was a distant relation of John Harden. He had been selling negroes from Tennessee; he soon made us know, and we soon made him know, that we were all of the same family; we then conversed freely. He told us that he was clear—that he had sold out, and was overrun with money. We told him we had one darkey on hand; he said he would go with us and look at our negro; and did go. He told the negro that he lived in Cincinnati; was agent for an Abolition society, and that he would like to take him there. The negro agreed, and was very anxious. Harden then told Wages and myself that if we would deliver him the negro at Napoleon, Arkansas, he would give us one thousand dollars for him. We agreed, and the day was set to deliver him. Harden then told the negro that he had to go to Natchez, and would meet us at the mouth of the Arkansas river. We now disposed of our saddles and bridles, and took our negro and packs, and made for the Mississippi river at Vicksburg, where we got on a steamboat for Napoleon. We landed, and again set our darkey to picking out cotton. Harden came in a few days, paid the thousand dollars, and took the negro. He requested us to remain there a few days. We made him a bill of sale in the name of the negro's master—Smith, by which name I passed. Wages passed as Mr. Jones and Harden by the name of John Newton. He was the same man that afterward, in 1843, murdered old Robert Lott. Harden then went with me to take his negro. I told the negro that his master had just landed in pursuit of him, and that he must go with Mr. Newton; it was his only chance to escape; that if he was found we should all be hanged, and he carried back to Texas. He agreed, and Harden went up the Arkansas river about twenty-five miles and sold the negro for twelve hundred and fifty dollars; got a draft on New Orleans for his money, payable in ninety days; was gone only four days, and returned to Napoleon.

Wages and I then informed him of our contemplated trip to Louisiana, about Christmas, and consulted with him as to the mode of operation. He and Wages both agreed in opinion, and Harden suggested to us that the best plan would be to go to Cincinnati and procure a good skiff, large enough to carry twenty persons, and fit her out with six row-locks and six good oars; pretend her for a peddling boat on Red river; lay in some whiskey, bacon, flour and other articles to trade upon; and have the boat towed down to the mouth of Red river or Bayou Sara; land the freight; take the first Red river boat up to Shreveport; there fit out the skiff and go up the river trading, until the opportunity to steal the negroes is offered.

This arrangement understood, Harden proposed to join us; go to Cincinnati with us, and take chances. We all took the first boat that passed, the "Tribune," bound to Pittsburg, and passed Louisville and landed in Cincinnati the ninth day. We immediately made a contract to have the skiff built; it was to be ready in two weeks, and was to be large enough to carry twenty-five barrels of freight, and to be long and narrow, so as to row swift. During the time the boat was building, we made some purchases of whiskey, flour, bacon and other produce, and during our stay in Cincinnati we all pretended to be strong Abolitionists, attended several private meetings, and formed acquaintance with several free negroes, to whom we communicated our intention to steal the seven negroes near Shreveport, and bring them to Cincinnati. They very much approved the idea. We then proposed for two of them to go with us and assist in bringing the negroes away. There were two of them, that had been employed as stewards on board of steamboats, that agreed to go, and they took situations on a steamboat for that purpose.

Our skiff being finished and all accounts settled, we contracted with the captain of a steamboat on which our two free darkies were employed, to take our freight and tow our skiff to Bayou Sara. The passage was long, on account of low water. We arrived at Bayou Sara about the tenth of November, and landed our freight and skiff. Wages and I stopped; Harden and the two free negroes went on. Harden to get his draft accepted, and the free darkies to get on a Red river boat; and they were all to make an arrangement for a boat bound to Shreveport, to call and take us and our freight.

After they left, Wages went to see our old friend, Mr. Welter, relative to the arrangement and disposal of our two free darkies. An arrangement was soon made, for our old friend W., knew the ropes too well to hesitate long.

About the twentieth of November a small steamboat landed (on board were Harden and our two darkies,) which had been specially employed to take our freight. We shipped our freight and took the skiff in tow and put off. On the way up, Wages, Harden and I made the necessary arrangement for our future plan of action. Harden was to go with us to Shreveport, and there feign himself sick; and let Wages and I take our two darkies in the skiff and our freight, and start up the river. Accordingly, we reached Shreveport about the fifth of December, and Harden was taken sick; Wages and I hurried our darkies, loaded our skiff and left for up the river. We went up the river to the ferry we had crossed with McGrath, and there we stopped. I went to selling, sometimes to Indians, sometime to whites, and very often to negroes. Wages procured a horse and saddle and put out in pursuit of McGrath, and found him at the house of the old Methodist that owned the seven negroes we were after. McGrath was sick; had been very sick; but was then able to walk about and take occasional rides. Wages and McGrath got an opportunity to have a private interview for a few minutes. They were to meet the next day on the road, five miles from that place. Wages staid all night, paid his bill next morning and left after breakfast, enquiring for some stray mules. McGrath started for the residence of a brother Methodist, some ten miles distant—

and they both met at the place appointed and held their consultation.

The negro camp meeting had been already appointed, about ten or twelve miles above Shreveport and about two miles from the river. Wages and McGrath having fully understood how to act, Wages told him where the boat could be found, ten days before Christmas, and they parted, and Wages returned.

Accordingly, at the time appointed, McGrath was at the boat. We had him and his horse provided for; he was made acquainted with our two free darkies, and all things were arranged and understood well that night. McGrath left next morning to prepare for the camp meeting, which was to commence in eight days. We loitered away our time; and two days before the commencement of the camp meeting, we dropped our skiff to a landing opposite the camp ground, where we lay trading. We had sold almost everything we had.

On the morning of the commencement of the meeting, we set our two free darkies over the river, and they went to the place early in the day. Wages and I cleared out our skiff of all barrels, boxes and dunnage of every description, and had everything in complete trim, row locks, oars and all ready. The meeting commenced. We had instructed our free darkies to what landing place to conduct these seven negroes we were stealing; and on the first night of the meeting, sure enough, they all came to us. Their master had furnished them with two mules and a wagon, to haul their bedding, etc., to the camp ground, and they had brought all their clothing, bedding, and everything they had. They informed us that they had sold all their poultry and crop, and had got money to support them for the year. They had procured another negro to drive the mules and wagon back to the camp ground; and by nine o'clock that night we were under way down stream.

## WELTER AND HARDEN'S DECEPTION—WELTER ACTING AS UNITED STATES MARSHAL.

We rigged all six of the oars; one of the women pulled one oar and I pulled one; Wages sometimes spelled me, and I would steer the boat, and the women would sometimes spell each other, and we run at the rate of about ten miles an hour. About eleven o'clock that night we passed Shreveport, and before day sometime, we passed Natchitoches, the point we were striving to make, for we knew there was a bayou about five miles below, where we could hide ourselves and skiff through the day. We put into the bayou a little before day, and at daylight we landed our skiff in some bushes and high grass, and we all went on shore in a thick palmetto swamp, built a good fire, cooked and eat, and drank good whiskey and every one slept what they wanted; and about sunset we left and rowed into the river again. By this time they all had got themselves more accustomed to rowing, and made better headway and with more ease. We run on in the night and lay-by in the day; and the third night we reached the mouth of Red River and lay in the swamp that day; and the fourth night, about midnight, we reached Tunica, and run our skiff in a creek just above; made a fire in the swamp and remained till daylight. After daylight sometime, we eat breakfast and Wages and I made an excuse to go to the village of Tunica to buy some cigars, and to get some eggs, etc. The negroes set us over with the skiff; we went down to the village and went to the tavern. There we found our old friend, Welter, and Harden, and three other men whom Welter introduced us to as his friends and acquaintances, but they were in fact his "strikers." Harden immediately after we left him at Shreveport, had gone down the river to Welter's and informed him where to meet us.

We held a consultation as to the best plan to pursue, and we all finally agreed that the safest and best plan was to let

Welter take all the negroes and pay us for them. He was to pay Harden for the two free fellows one thousand dollars in cash and his note for one thousand payable in six months. He was to pay Wages and I for our seven negroes and the skiff with all the apparatus, eight hundred dollars in cash and his note for four thousand dollars, payable in six months. After this arrangement was concluded Wages and I went to the skiff, took our guns to go a hunting, and then returned to the village. About two hours before sunset Welter took Harden and his three men, got a small boat and went up to the creek where all the negroes were. But before they got to the place they tied Harden's hands behind him to make the negroes believe that he was a prisoner for negro stealing. Welter and his men surrounded the camp and took all the negroes prisoners, and then brought up Harden tied. Welter then informed the two free negroes that he was the United States Marshal, and that it was his duty to take them and Harden back to Shreveport, where they would be tried for the crime of negro stealing, and that the punishment would be death or the penitentiary for life; but that he did not know that he could prove Harden guilty, and then asked them if Harden had been with them. They declared he had not. Welter then told the negroes that he knew them; that they had been stolen once before and sold in Louisiana, and that he knew all about them, and made them confess the truth. He then told the free negroes that their case was a desperate one; that it would be impossible for them to escape; and then asked them which they would prefer, to stand their trial or be sold as slaves for life. They said they had rather be sold as slaves; so he tied their feet, after putting them in the boat, and took in all their dunnage, and the other seven negroes. Upon their positive declaration that Harden was not concerned he was released, and a little after dark they rowed down to the village. Welter placed his three "strikers" to guard the boat and negroes, while he and Harden went on shore, and we all went into a private room in the tavern, where

C—5

we executed bills of sale for the negroes, dated them in Buncombe county, N. C., and signed fictitious names and witnesses. Welter paid us our money according to contract and executed the notes, after which we took a good supper together and drank three or four bottles of wine, and Welter left us. We went with him nearly to his boat and bid him good-by and good luck, and he rowed off down the river for home. Wages, Harden and I returned to the tavern, went to our room and to bed and slept very sound. Next morning we arose much refreshed, and greatly relieved in mind. We went very early to a coffee house, took a cup of coffee and our bitters, and returned to our room to consult as to the best course to pursue. We concluded to leave in the first boat for Natchez. We accordingly got breakfast, paid our bills and placed our guns and baggage at the nearest depot to the landing. We had to wait till late in the day before we could get a boat. We at last saw one coming, and procured a skiff to put us on board. At a signal the boat rounded to, and we went on board, registered our names (all fictitious) and paid our passage to Natchez.

### WAGES' AND HARDEN'S PLOT TO KILL ROBERT LOTT AND THOMAS SUMRALL.

When we landed at Natchez we all stopped at different hotels, but while there, some ten days, we had interviews and consultations every day. It was then that Wages and Harden made the plot to kill old Thomas Sumrall and old Robert Lott, and for that purpose Wages furnished Harden a map of all the roads in Perry county, Miss. Harden then informed us that he had a partner in Tennessee by the name of Goodwin, and that he expected Goodwin had, in a cave in the Cumberland mountains, several negroes then waiting for him to run off and sell, and that he must go up with the first rise of water so as to come down with the spring freshet. We all then made an arrangement to meet in New Orleans at a certain place on the Fourth of July coming, so as to collect our money from Welter, and for Harden to get the money on his draft for the negro sold on the Arkansas river, which he had deposited in bank for collection.

Our ten days in Natchez having expired, Harden and I took passage on a steamboat, Harden for Tennessee, and I for Vicksburg to await the arrival of McGrath. Wages was to be at Vicksburg in three or four days. I landed at Vicksburg; Harden went on. I went to one of the hotels, put up and waited for McGrath. On the sixth day Wages came, and went to another hotel, and we both waited there another week and still no McGrath. We began to get uneasy. However, three or four days after, I was standing on the bank of the river, when I saw a man dressed in coarse negro clothing, black and ragged, an old flapped hat, a pair of old saddle-bags on his arm and a big stick in his hand. He came up to me to inquire the road to Jackson. I did not know him at first, but he soon made me know him. It was McGrath. He inquired for Wages; I told him Wages was there; I told him to go to the cheapest boarding house, which he did, and his appearance caused him to have to pay his dollar in advance. That night we all got together, Wages, McGrath and myself; we went below the city and had a long consultation. We told McGrath what we had done, and gave him a full history of Harden and his two free negroes, and where Harden had gone, etc. He next gave us a detail of his voyage through the camp meeting and since, up to that time.

He said the next day after the seven negroes had left the camp ground he saw their mules and wagon, and no person appeared to be about them. A very likely young negro watered and sometimes fed the mules, and on the second day he went to the negro and asked what had become of the negroes that came with that wagon and mules. The boy answered first he did not know, and looked confused. He then said to the negro to tell him the truth and he would keep the secret and not expose him; the negro then told him the whole truth about the matter, and then asked McGrath's advice. He told him to take care of the mules and wagon until the meeting broke up, and then take them to their owner, and inquire of him why his negroes went off and left their mules and wagon so long, and not return at all, and give him the trouble to bring them home; and if any person attempted to whip him to make him tell anything about the matter he was to run away, and on the next Sunday night to meet him, McGrath, at a certain place and he would tell him what to do, and to be sure and keep everything a profound secret.

### MR. MOORE AFTER PREACHER M'GRATH, IN TEXAS.

With this understanding the meeting went on until the sixth day; the meeting broke up; the negro geared up his mules to the wagon and rolled off; drove them to the house of the owner and reported himself. It was late in the night. The old gentleman told him to feed the mules, get his supper and come to him in the morning and tell him more about it. The next morning the boy told the old man that he did not know but one of his negroes, and that was the fellow that asked him to feed and water the mules a day or two, and on the third day the negro did not return, and he asked the advice of one of the preachers, who told him to take them home. The old man asked the boy where that preacher was, and the negro said he was sick at a house about six miles from there. He then asked the boy who he belonged to, and the negro showed him his "pass," which told the truth. He then dismissed the boy and sent him home, and about ten o'clock, McGrath said, "here comes the old man." He rode up to the gate and hailed, and inquired if Brother McGrath was there. They told him he was. He alighted from his horse, came into the house and said good morning, very short. "Well, Brother McGrath, how do you do?"

"Oh, I am very sick, Brother Moore."

"What seems to be the matter?"

"Oh, I have caught a cold, and have a very severe pain in my side; I think it is side pleurisy."

"Well," said he, "did you see anything of my negroes at your meeting?"

McGrath told him: "I saw them there the first day with you when we went. After you left, Brother Moore, I don't recollect seeing them, and I thought you had ordered them home until I was asked by a strange negro what he should do with the mules and wagon. When I examined them I saw they were yours, and I told the negro to drive them to you and report himself. I would have gone with him, but was too unwell and had to stop here."

"Well," says the old man, "your great meeting has caused me to loose seven negroes, I fear."

McGrath said: "Oh, I hope not, Brother Moore."

"Yes it has!" said he very short, "and I wish there never had been a camp meeting in the world: and I know," said he, "they are stolen, and they went by water. Some of them picayune steamboat captains have stolen them, and they are now in Florida or Georgia. I will go and make some inquiry in Shreveport, and along the river, to find out what boats left about that time, and," said he, "I will go to the owner of that negro that brought the wagon home and have him tied up and whipped till he tells the truth about it, for I believe he knows all about the matter." McGrath said he tried to pacify the old gentleman, but it was all no go, so the old gentleman left.

McGrath said the times then were beginning to be rather squally. He pretended to improve very fast; was able to ride in two days, and set out to help Brother Moore hunt and track his negroes. On the next Sunday night he was at the place where he was to meet the negro, and the negro was there also. McGrath told of the threats against him, and asked him if he wished to run away and go with him, if he did he would find him a good master, or take him to a free State. The negro said he would go. McGrath asked him if he could steal a good horse, saddle and bridle. The negro said he could. McGrath then asked him if he could get over Red river and meet him at a certain place on a certain day. He said he could, three or four days after.

McGrath then went to the house of Brother Moore to inquire if he had got any tidings of, or from his negroes. The old man was very mad and talked very short, and said "no," adding: "Mr. McGrath, I want you to leave my house, and never again set your foot in it." McGrath tried to reason with the old man, but all would not do, so he left. He had collected among the brethren some five hundred dollars or upward and a considerable sum from the negroes at the camp meeting. He then went to Shreveport and procured some articles he wanted (and among them two half gallon jugs, one full of brandy and the other of whiskey), some bread and cheese, and crossed the river.

After he got across he saw three men come down to the ferry and wait for the ferryman; he watched them; they conversed with the ferryman awhile and rode back. McGrath rode on three or four miles, came to an inn and stopped. It was not night, but he had come to the conclusion now, that it was necessary for him to watch as well as pray. A little after dark up rode three men, and inquired if a travelar had passed that evening, and what time—how long before dark? They were informed none had passed; one had put up, a little before dark. They alighted and came in; enquired from McGrath his name, where he was traveling, his occupation, etc. He told his name, and said he was going to a quarterly meeting, some seventy-five miles from that place. They listened to him with keen, shrewd looks and very doubting air, and McGrath saw from their manœuvres that they were after him in particular, and he well knew it would require his best skill and ingenuity to evade their vigilance. They bid him good night and started on. McGrath pretended to walk out carelessly and watch them; they turned back.

He started next morning and traveled about thirty-five miles and stopped for the night. Just before night, the same three men passed the house. Next morning, after breakfast, he started again, and in a few miles came to their camp. "Well," said one, "we have met again." McGrath said "yes," and asked them which way they were going. They said to purchase beef cattle, and asked him how much further he was going that route? He told them he was going to a missionary station to see the preacher there; that it was about forty miles there, and he wanted to get there that night. He bid them good morning, road off, and traveled slow until he got out of their sight, and then pushed and rode about twelve miles. He came to a cross road that passed near where the negro was; here he left the road in a direction opposite to where the negro lay; tied his horse in a thicket some distance from the road, and concealed himself to watch. The men soon came to the place and examined for the track of his horse; they finally took the road which the horse's track had followed and pushed on. He went to where his horse was, stripped him, held him to graze some cane, and took a little of his good brandy; stripped his Methodist coat off and rolled up his broad-brimmed beaver in it and tied them on his saddle; and put on a common oiled cap, and another coat. Night came on; he saddled his horse and rode through the woods, near the road, to the distance of about two miles from where the negro was to meet him, and tied his horse about two hundred yards from the road. After it was fully dark, he started on the road on foot and left his horse, for the place appointed to meet the negro; and his only fear then was that the negro might have been bribed to betray him. He had two good single-barrelled pistols, and would be certain to save two of his assailants and take chances with the balance. He went on, got within a very short distance of the place appointed, crept up very close and stopped to listen. All was still. He discovered, a short distance from him, a large tree and a thick bunch of bushes around it. He crept easily to that, and squatted down at the root of the tree to listen. He thought he heard a stick crack or break close to him. He then gave a low whistle like that of a bird; it was answered immediately, within twenty feet of him. He then gave another, which was as promptly answered. He then gave a slap of his hands, which was answered, and the negro advanced to him. He asked the negro if there was any person about, and where was his horse? The negro told him about two hundred yards from there.

They started and went about half way, and McGrath stopped and told the negro to go and bring his horse there. The negro went and brought his horse. McGrath said he then became better satisfied that the negro was no traitor, and told him to go with him to the road and ride about thirty yards behind, until they got opposite where his horse was, which he did. They were not long in getting there. When we got to the place, he made a signal, and the negro rode up, and McGrath turned square off from the road and told the negro to follow him. He went about one hundred yards and told the negro to tie his horse and go back and watch the road, until he saddled and brought his horse. When McGrath had saddled his horse and returned, he found the negro at his horse, with everything ready to mount and be off. He asked what was the matter? "My God, master! we have had good luck; just as I went up close to the road I heard horses' feet, and hid in the bushes; I saw by starlight three persons pass the road; two of them I could see had guns, and if we had been ten minutes later we should have met them." McGrath pulled out his little jug of whiskey and gave the negro two drams and took one himself; they mounted their horses and started. He instructed the negro to travel about thirty yards behind in case of surprise, so as to make his escape and save them both.

They traveled hard that night, and by daylight they had made near sixty miles. At daylight they left the road and lay-by that day. It happened that the negro had near a half bushel of corn, and some meat and bread, and McGrath some bread and cheese, so they made out pretty well that day. Night came on and they set out again, and traveled until near day. They arrived close to a ferry on the Washita. Before getting there, they left the road a short distance, and McGrath left the negro with the horses and went towards the ferry. As he got near the ferry house, which he intended to go round, some person hailed—"who is that?" He turned his course and made back for the negro and horses. He had not time to get away before they passed in pursuit, and he heard them say, "that damned preacher is here somewhere, and we will have him yet." They halted a moment, and he heard their horses' feet, some going back and some the other way. McGrath mounted his horse and told the negro to follow him, and he took to the woods and steered a west course, which he knew was up the river, and traveled till he reached high land, and continued after day until near twelve o'clock, sometimes in sight of plantations, which he would go round.

By and by he came to a road that had the appearance of being much traveled, and leading north. Here, some distance from the road, he halted, stripped their horses and let them graze in a cane brake, and remained there till dark without anything to eat. At dark they started and traveled ten or twelve miles, passed several houses, and came to a house and passed down a hill into a lane, and at a short distance came to high timber land, which he knew was near the river. He stopped and left the negro with the two horses, giving him instructions if any alarm was heard, to turn and run back to a little branch and stop till he came. He went on to the river, and luckily there was no spy there, and the ferry-flat was on his side. He hurried back, took his horse and the negro and his horse, and got into the ferry-flat and went over. They mounted their horses and traveled until daylight; passed several houses and plantations. At daylight he found himself bordering on the Mississippi swamp. He turned off the road and stripped their horses to graze in a cane-brake.

Nothing to eat now for two nights and one day, with plenty

of money, but was afraid to go to a house, for fear of discovery.

He went to waylay the road, saw no person pass except emigrants, from whom we obtained a little bread, some salt and a small piece of meat. He inquired of them the road and distance to Vicksburg. They told him from seventy-five to one hundred miles. He inquired if they had met any person on horseback. They said no. He then left them and returned to his negro and horses; found the negro had killed a large, fat possum, and had it cleaned and was roasting it; the salt he had got then came in play. They cooked and eat, drank their liquor, and rested that day. A little before night McGrath went to the road to examine if any horses' tracks passing toward Vicksburg could be seen. There were none. He returned and saddled his horses, and a little before sunset they started and traveled all night, and until next day at ten o'clock. They came to the Tensas Bayou, crossed at a ferry, and inquired of the ferryman, who was a negro, how far it was to Vicksburg? The negro said about thirty miles. McGrath then inquired if there were many settlers on the bayou. The negro said there were plenty up and down the bayou on both sides. They left the ferry and went on a few miles, and turned to the west from the main road, up the bayou, along a new road that carriages had traveled, and went about ten miles—passed several large plantations. About twelve o'clock he came to the house of a small farmer; his horses were very tired, and he asked if he could get his horses fed and some dinner for himself and boy. The man told him to alight; the horses were soon attended to, and dinner was soon prepared and they eat.

McGrath then told the man he was from Mississippi; the negro he had with him was all he had; that they were about to sell him for a security debt; that he had to run him to save him; and that he had to travel a long distance and was much fatigued, both himself and horses, and that he would like to rest himself and horses a few days. This was agreed to. He then told the landlord that he was fearful they might follow him and that he did not wish to let many people know that he was there. He also told him that he would like to sell his negro, if he could get a good master for him, and that he would like to sell his two horses and go home by water, by way of New Orleans, Mobile and up the Tombigbee river. He also promised his landlord, if he would help him, and effect a good sale of his negro and horse, that he would make him a present of one hundred dollars, and that the negro might work in his farm while they were looking around. This was also agreed to, and it was concluded to rest the horses a week.

McGrath and the landlord (Mr. Chance was his name) rode up the bayou to see a blacksmith that wanted to purchase a negro. They traveled about thirty miles; saw the man and made a conditional trade with him, to sell him the negro for thirteen hundred and fifty dollars, if the negro could "blow and strike" in the shop, which the negro said he could. They then returned to Chance's, took the negro and the two horses and returned to the blacksmith. He tried the negro one day and said he was satisfied, and paid McGrath his money. The negro then told his new master to buy the horse that he had ridden; there was no better horse in the world. The master inquired the price; McGrath told him two hundred dollars; but as he had bought the negro he might have the horse for one hundred and seventy-five dollars. The blacksmith told him he would have to borrow one hundred and twenty-five dollars, but he knew where he could get it if they would wait until the next day; and he thought he knew a man that would give two hundred dollars for McGrath's horse. They consented to wait, and sure enough the next morning quite early the blacksmith returned with the money and a man with him, who soon closed the trade with MrGrath for his horse, and they paid him the money for the two horses, saddles and bridles, three hundred and seventy-five dollars, making the whole sum seventeen hundred and twenty-five dollars. McGrath gave the negro one hundred dollars as a present, and asked him if he was satisfied. He said he was well satisfied. McGrath and Mr. Chance they left for Chance's residence, which they reached that night.

### M'GRATH IN DISGUISE.

On their way down McGrath made a bargain with Chance to carry him in his little wagon to the ferry opposite Vicksburg, for fifteen dollars. The next day he paid Chance one hundred and fifteen dollars; made the landlady, Mrs. Chance, a present of ten dollars for her trouble; and after dinner they started for Vicksburg landing. He told Chance he wished to travel in disguise for fear he might be followed, and for that purpose Chance procured for him a negro's old jacket and trowsers, and an old flapped hat and Chance's old saddle bags; "and in this garb," said McGrath, "I landed on the other side of the river last night and camped there with my friend Mr. Chance. We parted early this morning, he for home, and I for this place; and here I am this 25th day of January, 1841, and" said he, "I have kept a regular diary of my travels ever since we parted on Red River, before the camp meeting," and he showed us his memorandum book.

Now, Wages, McGrath and I had all got together again. We had realized over twenty five thousand dollars by our hypocrisy, stealing, burning and murdering. We advised McGrath to change his clothes and put on a genteel suit, and procure a pair of green goggles, so as to disguise himself, and we repaired each to our hotels. The next day McGrath came out in a new suit, with his green goggles, and we should not have known him ourselves, had we not been on the look out for him. He came to the same hotel where I boarded. We advised McGrath to leave in the first boat for St. Louis, where we were to meet him on a certain day; but each of us was now to travel in separate boats. McGrath set out the next day;

two days after Wages left; and one day after that I took a boat, and we all met at the time appointed. We remained in St. Louis a few days, and changed our clothing to that of common laborers.

## MURDER OF O'CONNOR ON THE MISSISSIPPI RIVER.

We all took passage on a steamboat bound from St. Louis to Pittsburg; landed at the mouth of the Wabash, and traveled up that river to the town of............, where we fell in with an old Irishman by the name of O'Connor. He was a western trader, and had two large flat boats loaded with flour, bulk pork, onions, potatoes, butter, some whiskey, and a variety of other articles, to the amount of over five thousand dollars.

With him McGrath soon formed acquaintance, and came the "country" over him. His brother Irishman, McGrath, represented to him that our occupation was that of working flatboats; and that we had made many trips from Missouri, Indiana, Illinois and Ohio. We were not long in making a contract with him, to help him down with his boats. He had contracted for one hundred barrels of whiskey, which he could have if he could pay five hundred dollars. We advanced him some money and he made the purchase and gave his note for the balance. We put the whiskey on board the boats, and all things being ready we set off down the river.

He employed two extra hands to help us down to the mouth of the river, where he discharged them. We went on down, two hands on each boat, until we passed the shoal at Smithland, the mouth of the Cumberland river, when we lashed the two boats together and took our watches by turns, two at a time. We floated all one day and part of a night, and came to the mouth of the Ohio, between midnight and daylight.

It was the turn for Wages and I to take the watch that morning. Now, on the Mississippi River, all we had to do was to keep the boats in the middle of the stream, with a light on deck to guard against steamboats. The old Irishman, the owner of the boats, went down into a small cabin in one of the boats, which he had prepared for himself, and laid down in his berth to sleep. He was much fatigued, but before he went to sleep, Wages proposed to him to take a dram of stewed whiskey punch, hot, which he knew to be a favorite beverage with the Irish. The old man consented, and Wages went to work to prepare it. We being on the alert for any and everything, had the opium ready, and gave his bowl a full charge. He drank it down and praised it as very nice, and retired. We then prepared some punch for ourselves and drank it. We then went to an opposite end of the boats and held a consultation, as to who was to make way with the old man, and it fell to my lot to strike the fatal blow!

Oh, God! when I look back, it makes me shudder. Even now it chills the blood in my veins.

It was understood that the deed was to be committed at sunrise, precisely, provided there were no boats of any kind near. By the time we had accomplished our consultation, daylight was making its appearance in the east, and I cannot here describe my feelings. Wages and McGrath discovered my embarrassment, and resorted to another potion of hot whiskey punch, which I drank freely. After I had drank, I went into the old man's cabin, armed with a small hatchet or lathing axe. The old man was fast asleep, lying on his back; I went up on deck and looked to the east, and saw that the sun was just making his appearance; I returned to the little cabin, raised the hatchet and struck the fatal blow in the centre of the forehead, a little above the eyes. It made a full dent in the skull the size of the hammer of the axe. He utter a kind of suppressed and strangled shriek and in a very few minutes O'Connor was numbered among the dead.

Now the next business was to dispose of him. This, however did not take us long, for we had some old cast iron grates, that had belonged to a steamboat and which we used to set our cooking pots on. We took two of them and lashed them well together, stripped off his clothing and left his body naked, and tied a strong rope around his neck, and attached that to the cast iron grates.

And oh! the awful scence that ensued! To see a fellow-being who had been one of us so recently; to see his body cast to oblivion, and his soul, then departed, to that "bourne from whence no traveler returns." Well, or not well it was, I may say. Poor old O'Connor went down with about three hundred pounds of iron attached to him—a little below Wolf Island, not far from Mills' Point.

We very soon passed New Madrid. On our way down the Mississippi we had several calls of "What boat is that?" "Where are you from?" to which we replied the "Non Sach," and "Red Rover," from "Independence, Mo."

Our next business was to dispose of his clothing, his papers, and to so disfigure the boats that they could not be identified. So we took the same "hatchet," and rubbed off "Non Such" and "Red Rover," and wrote in their place "Tip," and "Tyler," which in those days took well. Thus rigged out, we glided on gently and steadily; we had nothing to fear; we had two flat-boats, and they well loaded with produce, worth over five thousand dollars.

To dispose of the boats and cargo was our next business, we well knowing that other boats would be down from the same river inquiring for O'Connor's boats. We therefore lost no time. We never stopped till we came to the mouth of Red river, where we halted and warped into the mouth and tied up. McGrath mounted his green gozzles, blacked his hair and face, so that I could not have known him, only that I was with him. Wages took one of our skiffs and went to Tunica, where he took a steamboat down to Welter's. In a few days he and Welter returned, and we were not long in closing a trade with him. He gave us four thousand five hundred dollars in his note payable the Fourth of July ensuing for our boats and cargo. One boat was sent down the Atchafalya bayou, and the other down the Mississippi to his residence.

Wages and Welter returned to Welter's, and McGrath and I remained to take care of the boats. A day or two after Welter sent four of his "strikers" to take charge of the boats; and after dividing the cargoes, one of them left down the river for Welter's with two of his men on board. We remained on the other until we got an opportunity to have it towed into the Atchafalya bayou, and we then made the best of our way down the river to Welter's, where we again joined Wages.

We there held a full consultation, and concluded to return to the vicinity of Mobile, lie still for a while, collect and gather up our money and secure it all at one place, where it could be easily got if we should stand in need of it at any time. This brought about the last of May, 1843. We went up to Natchez, landed there, and steered our course through the country by Liberty, Holmesville, Columbia, and on to Allen Brown's, on Red creek, in the southwest corner of Perry county, Miss., where Wages and I rested until about the last of June, when we started on foot and walked to Pass Christian.

There we took a steamboat to New Orleans; from there up the Mississippi to our old friend Welter's to fulfill our engagement with Harden on the Fourth of July. We arrived there on the 2d of July, at night. Harden had been there some day or two before us, dodging about rather concealed.

McGrath was either sick, or so feigned himself. We left him at Brown's, and in the neighborhood. Wages and I often talked about the matter, and we came to the conclusion that he was fearful of meeting some of his brother Methodists on some of the steamboats, and had concluded to keep out of the way. So Wages, Harden and I had a full conference relative to our future course of operations, and came to a final conclusion, and each made a short memorandum in his "diary" in our mystic characters on the evening of the 3d of July.

On the morning of the fourth, Welter informed us that he

and his family had an invitation to partake of a "public dinner and ball, and that he would like to invite us, but was afraid of the enquiries that would be made, of "who we were," "where we were from," and "what was our occupation," &c. He said, "there have been some enquiries about boat loads of produce, and where I purchased so many negroes, and I think we had better be more cautious for some time to come." He told us that he would furnish us a good dinner at his house and plenty of wine and liquors of the best, and we might enjoy ourselves until he returned next day. We accordingly lived well that day and night. The old gentleman returned with his family next day, about ten in the forenoon, and as he said, much fatigued.

"Now, gentlemen," said he, "the fourth of July is over; we will to business, if you are ready;" to which we replied, "we were like old souse, always ready!" "Now, your money is ready for you in New Orleans," says Welter, "and I will go down on the first boat that passes. You must all take separate boats; for," said he, "the times are squally in this region; the papers are full of rewards for those seven negroes, and there is also a reward for three men, who are supposed to have killed a flatboat man by the name of O'Connor; and if you three travel together you will be sure to be arrested; I will go first and have your money ready. Disguise yourselves as much as possible, and meet me in our rendezvous in four nights after to-night; and tell me what kind of money you want."

Harden told him "Tennessee bank notes would suit him;" Wages and I told him either Mobile Bank or Bank of Louisiana would do us.

Just at this moment his waiter came to tell him there was a boat in sight. He left immediately for the city. I tied up my head, rubbed some ink around one eye, and put a green silk patch over it, and took a boat the same evening; Harden the next morning; and Wages the evening after. We had our ap-

C—6

pointed boarding house, where we eat and slept in a private room, where no person but our landlord ever saw us.

At the appointed time Welter met us, and paid us our money. Harden his one thousand dollars and Wages and myself eight hundred dollars in Mobile and New Orleans money. After paying us all, he said: "Now, young men, let me advise you a little. You have done a storming business in your line. You have met with extreme success in everything you have undertaken, and I do assure you that the glass pitcher, in going to the fountain too often, will come back broken eventually; now let me advise you each to return to your homes and friends, collect and realise all your money and exchange it into gold or silver coin, and have it ready for any emergency; keep yourselves secluded as much as possible from the criticisms of the community in which you reside, and the time will wear around when you may turn loose again; but rest assured that I shall have to withdraw all connection with you for the present: my property is ample for the support of myself and family now, and a liberal division among them after I am dead; I wish you well, and hope you will act prudently for the future and not run too great risks." So saying he gave us each a hearty shake of the hand, and bid us a final adieu. This was our last interview with Welter. Since then we have not seen or heard from him.

Our understanding with Harden was that he was to return to the vicinity of Mobile in the fall or early in the winter. The next morning early Harden, Wages and I paid our landlord and left; Harden up the river to Tennessee, and Wages and I went to the New Basin, took passage on a wood freighting schooner to the Bay of St. Louis, and up Wolf river to a landing in the piney woods. We had provided ourselves with some biscuit, cheese and meat. We landed and walked to Allen Brown's again, where we landed the second night, very tired. McGrath, when we returned, was over on Black creek at Daniel Smith's, hard up courting his daughter, Mary Smith, whom he married the next June following. He soon got the word that Wages and I had returned, and came over to Brown's.

Now we were all easy, with plenty of time to feast and frolic. We soon sent off to Pass Christian for flour, sugar, coffee, and whiskey, too, tobacco, cigars, and other little nicknacks. We first tried our hand at hunting deer and fishing in Red creek, and did kill a few deer and caught some fish, but we found that too fatiguing in that hot season, and we resorted to other means to procure our fresh meat. And the way we slung old Bill Griffin's fine fat heifers and yearlings was a caution. Their meat was very fat and remarkably fine flavored.

We remained at Brown's and in the vicinity until after the middle of August, and I don't believe that old Brown and his family had ever lived so well in his or their lives before. It was then that Wages commenced courting old Brown's daughter, whom he afterward married; and it was then that Brown made the proposition to Wages to go into the "counterfeiting business;" and I am here compelled to say that the association of Allen Brown with us was the main cause of our exposure, the death of Wages and McGrath, and the annihilation of our clan, and the prime cause of my fate.

Well, we rusticated at Brown's our time out, and all of us were fully satiated to our heart's content, and now the time had arrived for us to leave for our places near Mobile. A small consultation as to the way of our departure was necessary, and as McGrath was a member of the church, and had made frequent visits to Brother Smith's and Brother Bounds, he could go publicly any way, and was to go by way of the back Bay of Biloxi to visit the brethren about Evans', while Wages and I prepared ourselves with three days provisions, and started one moonlight night—Brown with us, and two of his horses. He went with us about thirty miles that night, and left us in the morning and returned home. We lay by that day near the road, and started a little before sunset and crossed Pascagoula at Fairley's ferry before daylight next morning. We were then on our own native hills. We again laid by. The next night we crossed Dog river at Ward's bridge, and reached home early in the morning. McGrath arrived about ten days after us. Our first business was, after resting awhile, to gather all our money and have a correct settlement and distribution of our funds.

Now it was honor among thieves! I disgorged all into the hands of Wages; he said to McGrath that he knew I had given up all. "Now, McGrath," said Wages, "shell out." So McGrath did turn out the seventeen hundred and twenty-five dollars. Wages said to him "where is that gospel money?" to which McGrath replied that the amount was small, and that he thought he ought to retain that for pocket and spending money. Wages then came out upon him in plain terms, and said: "McGrath, you came in with us upon equal terms, and if you wish to bulk or fly back, take your seventeen hundred dollars and leave, but look out for the consequences!" McGrath soon forked over about thirteen hundred dollars more. We had, when properly estimated, thirty-one thousand eight hundred and seventy-five dollars. This money was in joint stock between us three, and a proper appropriation and distribution of that sum was what we had next to look to.

"Now," said Wages, "boys, we have this amount of money, part in possession, and the balance at command. Let us devise some plan to save it; this, however, you may reflect upon. Our next business is to get the whole in possession; when we have done that, our next business is to make the proper disposition of it. So now we have buried at one place four thousand five hundred dollars, and our deposits in bank in New Orleans six thousand six hundred and seventy-five dollars, and what we now have makes our account tally; our next business is to get it altogether. When we have done that we must reflect well; and," said Wages to me, "James, I would rather that you and McGrath would lie down and sleep until I have all that matter accomplished, for I am fearful of your youthful imprudence, and McGrath's imprudent Irish brogue to go in blind right or wrong, and always come out at the little end of the horn, as they did at Vinegar Hill, or as Mitchell, Meagher and others did in their recent effort in Ireland to obtain their liberty." I then proposed to McGrath to give Wages the whole and sole control, to which he finally consented, though, I discovered, with some reluctance.

"Now, boys," said Wages, "I wish you to consider yourselves upon the world until I return; and I enjoin on you not to commit any unlawful act during the time it may take to realize and gather together our money. For the certainty and uncertainty of life we cannot account; we will therefore deposit what money we have." So we did—in the ground—and each took fifty dollars for pocket money.

As the whole matter was now understood, McGrath returned to the back Bay of Biloxi, to preaching and stealing, and I remained in the vicinity of Mobile, pretending to burn and sell charcoal; but in fact stealing and feeding a parcel of our loafing and starving clan in Mobile, such as G. Cleveland, and some others of less importance that I could name, but whose names are not worth the pen, ink and paper it would take to write them.

But I will now tell you all about this man G. Cleveland, so far as I know him. When Wages, McGrath and I were in St. Louis, we fell in with this fellow Cleveland. We had seen him before in Cincinnati, but not to form an acquaintance. In St. Louis he was all the time around us—he may have smelt us out. He was then selling spurious money of "New York North River Bank, Schommerhorn, president," and several other banks of this same stripe. He traveled then in considerable style, with two large leather trunks, and they mostly packed with this spurious money. His portmanteau contained a great variety of "dickeys" and "collars," and his natural appearance and address always imposed upon a person unacquainted with him. Wages then advised me not to have anything to do with him, as he was a dangerous tool; and he so advised me until the day of his death, but not taking Wages' advice, Cleveland and his concern got out of me some three hundred dollars, with a faithful promise that I should be defended and protected; that jail doors, grates or bars should not hold me; but that they and their friends would burst asunder everything for me. Now see where his pledge falls. He and his whole concern will not flourish long. I have to suffer death solely for the want of a proper effort being made by them. I now leave Cleveland and the others to the mercy of their own conscience and the censure of the world.

Now to our affairs. Wages had returned to New Orleans, with all our money, and had purchased five barrels of whiskey, in one of which he had placed all the money. He had procured the whole of it in gold, and made a long, slim canvass bag, which he could pass through the bung-hole of the barrel, and in this bag he had placed his gold, mostly sovereigns, and five and ten dollar pieces of American coin. After placing the money in the barrel he put in the bung tight, and nailed on the tin; shipped it as an ordinary barrel of whiskey, and hauled it out to one of our camps, where we opened it, and took out the gold. We had on hand a considerable amount of bank notes of New Orleans and Mobile Banks. We then agreed that Wages should take it all, and exchange it for gold, under pretense of entering land for some company in Mississippi. Wages took his little two-horse wagon, loaded with pickets, and went to Mobile. The first trip he brought home near eight thousand dollars in gold, which was deposited with the rest. I then proposed to Wages and McGrath to make the amount in gold, thirty thousand dollars even, and bury it in some safe place, secure, so that we might have it for any emergency; and in case of the death of one of us, the other two were to share it; and if two died, one had all. So the next trip Wages made to Mobile, he brought the balance to make up the amount. We had three strong kegs made in

Mobile, well iron hooped, and we placed in each ten thousand dollars; filled all the crevices with clean, white sand, headed the kegs up, gave them three coats of paint, and after they were thoroughly dry, we buried them in a thick swamp on Hamilton's Creek. The balance of our money we then divided between us equally, which gave each share about six hundred and twenty-five dollars.

To accomplish our settlement of affairs, brought about the middle of November, 1843. McGrath left for the back Bay of Biloxi, and I saw nothing more of him until after his marriage.

About two weeks after, Harden arrived at Wages' riding a very fine horse, and had with him a likely mulatto fellow, riding on a very fine horse also, both of which he told me he sold to a man by the name of Jenkins. The first object to be effected was to kill and rob old man Sumrall. Mr. Newton was to turn preacher and go to Mr. Sumrall's house, and by some means effect the object; but by some misstep his intention was discovered through one of the house servants, the alarm was given, and brother Newton was ordered to leave brother Sumrall's premises. Wages and I lay in ambush, and had our appointed places to meet. We soon learned the result of Harden's adventure at Sumrall's. I returned to Mobile, Harden went to Louisiana, and Wages, by Jasper county, to Mobile. We were all to meet again about the last of February, on Black Creek, at the Pearlington road. We did meet, and a very few days after old Robert Lott was killed and all his money taken. This was sometime early in March, 1844. Wages was with Harden that night, and helped; I did not happen there. I met Wages next morning, at our camp, and he told me what was done, and turned me back. Harden and Wages had divided a little over two thousand dollars. Harden left a few nights after for the Mississippi swamp in Louisiana, and Wages and I for Mobile, and traveled altogether in the night, to avoid discovery.

## MEETING OF THE CLAN IN MOBILE, ALABAMA.

After we got to Mobile and had rested ourselves, there were several complaints made to Wages and I, about the derangement of the affairs of the clan. They had, during our absence, elected a president *pro tem*. Wages went round and called a meeting at the Wigwam. There was a crowded meeting, but they were mostly new members, who were very noisy. Wages then told them the object of the meeting; that it was to inquire into the situation of the clan; that his long absence had prevented him from attending any meeting for over two years; it was necessary to inquire into the affairs, and a system of action must be preserved in all institutions. Some of the new members were very clamorous and wanted to make a break and a raise at something; they had no money and must have some, and all such stuff. Wages then reminded them that we had a Vigilant Committee, who at all times had the control and power to report, and upon their report the clan would act. He also reminded them of their obligation and the terms upon which they came into the clan, and for any breach or exposure their life would pay the forfeit. He then announced to the meeting that he would hold an adjourned meeting that night two weeks, for the purpose of having the minutes made up, and a full report from the Vigilant Committee; but, before the time arrived, Wages was informed that four of these members had come in as spies, and that we had traitors in the ranks. He then advised me of the fact, and we agreed to withdraw. We never visited the Wigwam again; but we formed a new and select one among a few of us, and among the new clan were four of my brothers—Isham, nicknamed Whin, Henry, John and Thomas Copeland, Jefferson Baker and Joshua Walters, all men of bravery.

Our next business was to dispose of all spies and traitors, and it was not long before four of them butted their heads against a slung-shot hung to a man's arm, and they went floating from Mobile wharf down the channel of the river. Old Palmer, one of our clan, near Springhill, met up with my brother Whin and I; he had made some exposures of our affairs. Our two rifles made clear fire, and we left him in a situation where he told no more tales. Sometime after, Tom Powell, another of the clan, made some threats that he intended to drive the Copelands out of the country. McGrath and I waylaid him and fed him with the contents of two double-barrel shot-guns, about forty-eight buck-shot, and put him in a swamp near Eslaya's old mill. Another of the clan, Jim Harper, attempted to betray us by decoying us into the hands of some of our enemies; Wages, McGrath and I managed to catch him. We took him into an old house near the old Stage Stand. We then put a rope around his neck, and we very soon squeezed the breath out of him. We stripped off his clothes, and left him in the old house, a prey to the buzzards; took all the clothes some distance off and piled lightwood knots on them, and burnt them.

Sometime after McGrath was married, Wages went over into Mississippi, about old Brown's, and sometimes down about Honey Island, near Gainesville, and remained there from the summer of 1843 until the fall of 1844, during which time I had seen him but twice, when he came over to his father's on a visit. in the fall of 1844, Wages and McGrath came over to the vicinity of Mobile and sent for me, and then informed me of the plan they were about to pursue. That they were going to commence making counterfeit money; that they had procured a man who could engrave their dies, and another who was a professed chemist and could prepare the metal so well that it would take a very acute judge to detect it. I told Wages that whatever he went at I was in; "but," said I, "I feel somewhat fearful." "Oh," said they, "we have made a large acquisition to our clan, we now have Jim McArthur, Jack McArthur, Allen Brown, Daniel Brown, Jim Bilbo and Wash Bilbo. We are to settle McGrath at Honey Island;

Wages at Catahoula; Allen Brown at Red Breek, and the Bilbos and McArthurs are to range from Pearl River to Pascagoula; and, said they, "your party can range from Mobile to Pascagoula, and you can pass horses or negroes from Georgia to Florida on this route through to Louisiana, without discovery, and so from Louisiana in the same way." I then told Wages and McGrath both, that I was still afraid of their new acquisition. I then proposed to them to remove our money from Hamilton's Creek, and place it somewhere near where Wages was going to settle. I made this proposition because I believed that this counterfeiting business would be the means of getting us into trouble, and that we could procure our money more easily from that vicinity than we could where it was.

I had then arrived at the age of majority and began to have a more reflecting mind, and I never did have any reliance or confidence in that money arrangement. Wages then informed me that he was engaged to marry Allen Brown's daughter, but did not know what time: it might be a year before he did so. "McGrath," said he, "is now married, and will move to Honey Island shortly; I shall be engaged in preparing our shop and arranging the materials, and making preparations for the settlement of my home."

They then told me that Niel McIntosh, would also be one of our clan, and that he would travel to and from Mobile to our other places, as a spy, and look out for us. They left the next day for Mississippi, and I saw nothing more of either of them for over twelve months. Niel McIntosh made several trips over and back, and always had plenty of their money, but I was always afraid of it. He passed a considerable amount in the vicinity of Mobile, and made something by it.

John Harden brought three or four fine horses, one, he said, from Florida and the others from Georgia: I advanced him the money and passed them on to Wages, who sold them for me. S. Harden made two trips to the vicinity of Mobile that year, one from North Alabama, and one from western North Carolina: The first trip he brought two good horses and a likely negro boy. I assisted him to sell the horses near Fort Stoddart, for a fine price, to some men going to Texas. I then furnished him two ponies and sent McIntosh to pilot him through to Wages, who paid him for his negro and sent him to Pearlington, where he again embarked for Tennessee, by way of New Orleans.

About four months afterwards Harden returned again. He had two splendid horses, fine traveling equipage, and a likely mulatto girl about sixteen years old, dressed in boys clothes, traveling with him as his waiter. He said he had traveled through Georgia and Eastern Alabama to Blakely, and crossed the Bay over to Mobile, and came out to our place. He told us he feared no pursuit; that he had traveled too far, that there was no danger. I assisted him in selling the two horses, in Mobile, and saw them often afterwards. They were fine buggy horses. The girl he sold to a man in Mobile, who kept her as a wife, and she now passes for free. He had stolen her from a rich old widow lady in North Carolina, who had sent the girl on an errand, on a Saturday morning, some twenty-five miles on the same fine horse, to return on Sunday evening, and she never did return.

In these two trips of Harden's he gave me five hundred dollars for my assistance. I then assisted him to steal a very fine horse on the Tombigbee River, for which he gave me fifty dollars more, and left for Tennessee. This had pretty well consumed the fall of 1845.

In December, Wages came home to his father's; sent for me; told me that he was going to get married shortly, and invited me to his wedding; I promised him I would go if my business did not prevent me; but it so turned out that he did marry a short time after, and I was not present. After his marriage, he brought his wife to see his father and mother, and spent some weeks with them. He had with him plenty of counterfeit coin, and wanted me to take some and pass for him. That

I refused to do, and I then advised him that it would be better for us all to let that alone; and then reminded him that when there was none but him, McGrath and I together, that we could get along to better advantage, do a more profitable business and had a wider field to operate in. But he seemed to think that they could manage to get along; and I found from his conversation that old Allen Brown had got control of him, and I said no more on the subject. I told him frankly that their money I would have nothing to do with; but in other matters of stealing and selling horses, negroes and cattle, I would take a hand as heretofore, to which he assented, and here we dropped the subject for the present. I again urged upon him the removal of our money. I dreaded an outbreak, for I then believed that old Brown would blow the whole matter; and sure enough he afterwards did.

So Wages and his wife left, and went back to Mississippi, to old Brown, and he went to work building his house on Catahoula, in Hancock County. He got it completed; moved into it; took his horse; came again to Mobile; procured his father's two horse wagon to haul some articles for house-keeping from Mobile, and on his way back I went with him, the first night, and we camped near where our money was buried. We went and got the three kegs; placed them in the bottom of his wagon, covered them with hay and placed the balance of his load on them. He hauled them out to Hancock county, and deposited them in Catahoula Swamp, about a mile and a half or two miles from his house, and designated the place by a large pine tree that grew at the margin of the swamp, to the north-east, and about thirty-five yards from where the kegs were deposited, and a magnolia tree that grew about ten yards to the south-west. He gave me a diagram of the place, the courses, and distances which he had measured accurately, marked in lines and explained in our mystic key. That paper I somehow lost in the famous Harvey battle.

So it was Wages left and went to his place. Now he and

his crowd were for themselves, and me and my crowd for ourselves. My crowd consisted of myself, and four brothers, Josh Walters, Jef. Baker and old McIntosh, our outside striker, to run stolen horses or a negro, when required. Our range was from Mobile to Pascagoula, and from the Sea Coast to St. Stephen's. We fed ourselves and families upon pork, beef and mutton, in abundance, and we sold enough in the market to pay us from fifty to one hundred dollars per month—sometimes ready butchered and sometimes on foot, during the summer and fall season. Those we sold the meat of, we generally stole in the vicinity of Mobile. Old man Wages had a farm on Big Creek Swamp, about twenty-five miles from Mobile, in rather an obscure place. That was our place of resort and deposit, and many a stolen beef and horse has been concealed there until we could dispose of them.

We continued that business during 1845, 1846, and until the summer of 1847. We had stolen a small drove of cattle out near Chickasahay, and in driving them we gathered a few head near Mobile, belonging to old Moses Copeland. We sold the cattle to Bedo Baptiste, who paid my brother Henry and I for them. We claimed them; Whinn, or Isham and John helped to drive, but received none of the money. My brothers Henry and John, and Isham or Whinn, were arrested and tried. Henry was convicted of the larceny and served two years in the penitentiary of Alabama. Whin and John were acquitted; I took to the bushes. They did not catch me that hunt, and I lay in the woods and was concealed among my clan the balance of that summer, most of the time at old Wages', on Big Creek, waiting for Gale Wages to come so as to make a settlement with him, and to close my business and leave the country.

The time passed on slowly. I stopped all further operations until I could hear from Wages and McGrath, and, lo! some time late in the fall up rolled Wages and old Brown, and sure enough old Brown, as I had anticipated and expected, had blown the whole concern. He had gone into the little town of

Gainesville and passed a few dollars of their money for some small articles of trade, where the old fool might have known he would be detected; and sure enough he was. Now the next step was for him to get out of the difficulty, and when asked where he got the money, he said "from Bilbos." They were arrested and brought up, and he swore it on to them, and they had to give bail to answer the charge of passing counterfeit money.

Bilbos then swore vengeance against Brown and Wages, who had pulled up stakes and were leaving Hancock county, and Mississippi, too. The Bilbos pursued them, and passed them some way; turned back, and the parties met suddenly on a small hill. While one party ascended on one side the other party ascended on the other side, and both parties were within a few paces of each other at first view. Wages had the advantage of them; he had his double barrel gun well loaded and fresh caps on; Bilbos had their rifles well loaded and fresh primed, but they had a rag over the powder in the pan to keep it dry. These rags they had to remove before they could fire. Wages immediately fired and killed one of them dead, and then fired at the other before he could get ready to shoot and broke his thigh. From some cause Bilbo's horse got scared and threw him to the ground, and he immediately begged for his life. At first sight of the Bilbos old Brown ran, so Wages said.

Now it was that Wages and Brown both had to make their escape the best way they could. They came to Mobile, and there they were on the scout, as well as myself. McGrath was so well identified with them that he was watched very closely about Gainesville. He got into some corn stealing scrape, and broke into Hancock jail, and nothing but the gold or silver key ever turned him out. He and Wages happened to have a little of that, and he and his wife then left Honey Island, and were at Daniel Smith's, on Black creek, in Perry county. So it was Brown and Wages managed to get their families, and McGrath and his wife back into the vicinity of Mobile some time in November, 1847.

Wages and McGrath had very near got through with all their money. McGrath, in particular, had none, only as he borrowed. Wages had some, but had spent a large amount in feeding and clothing old Brown and his gang. Wages and his wife remained on Big creek at the old man's place, and I the greater part of the time with him. Brown and McGrath moved down on Dog river, near Stage Stand, pretending to burn coal and cut wood to sell, but they were in fact stealing, for they had nothing to eat and but little money. Brown had sold his possessions in Perry county to Harvey, and had received all his pay but forty dollars. He had represented his land to be saved or entered land, when it was public land, and Harvey refused to pay the forty dollar note, and that same pitiful note, and Brown's rascality and falsehood cost Wages and McGrath their lives, and Harvey and Pool their lives, and have placed me where I am.

Wages and I while on Big creek held a consultation as to our future course. Wages then sorely repented any connection that he ever had with old Brown, "and," said he, "I intend to get away from him, for I am fearful the old fool will get drunk and tell everything he does know." We then concluded our best way was for Wages to take his horse and cart, take old Niel McIntosh with him, and his wife and child, and start west and travel in the vicinity of Pearl river; there leave his wife; take the cart and horse and he and McIntosh to travel down Pearl river till they came opposite Catahoula; then turn in and get our money, and cross the Mississippi river; send McIntosh back to let McGrath and I know where to find him, and for us to slip off and go slyly, and not let Brown know where we were going, "and," said Wages, "if I can manage to rob old Tom Sumrall on my route and make a raise, so much the better. And you and your crowd may manage to make a raise here before you leave."

## BURNING OF ELI MAFFITT'S HOUSE, AND ATTEMPTED MURDER OF HIS WIFE.

The same day Wages and I were consulting thus, my brother John Copeland came to bring me some clothes, and he informed me that it was reported that old Eli Maffitt held a large amount of money, and that there was a project on foot to rob him and burn his house the first good opportunity; that Maffitt had taken a contract to build a bridge in Perry county, and would shortly leave home, and that Eli Myrick was to let the party know what time Maffitt commenced the bridge and would be absent from home. I then told Wages what was on foot. He then said "let me leave home about three days before, and I will try on the same night to rob old Sumrall and burn his house." In a few days Myrick came down and told us that Maffitt was up in Perry county, and would not be home in two weeks. Wages immediately geared up, and started with his cart, his wife and McIntosh. Three nights after that Allen Brown, McGrath, John Copeland and I went to Maffitt's just after dark, about seven o'clock, on the night of the 15th of December, 1847. Eli Myrick did not go with us, because he said Mrs. Maffitt would know him too well, but he was in the secred and shared his part of the money.

On getting near, we stopped to consult as to the safest way to get the money. Some were for robbing the house and not injuring any of the family. That I opposed, for I never believed in leaving any living witness behind to tell what I had done, if there was any way to prevent it. I always thought that two persons were enough to keep a secret, and it was safest if one of them were dead, for dead witnesses give no evidence. It was agreed that we should go into the house and demand the money, and if given up, to leave the inmates peaceably and unharmed.

John and I went in with a very stern look, thinking we could frighten the old lady, and make her give up every dollar that was in the house. But we were as sternly and peremptorily refused. The old lady said that she knew nothing about the money, and if she did, that we would not get it; we then told her that we had come after money and that money we would have before we left that house, or her life; and she still bravely defied us. John Copeland had in his hand a large hickory stick and I had another. Perceiving that she was determined, and our only chance to get the money was to kill her, while the old lady and I were quarreling about the money, I gave my brother John the wink, and he struck her a blow on the head which felled her to the floor. He repeated the blows, and I hit her several blows. We were then certain that we had killed her. We then commenced plundering the house, in search of the money; and we ransacked the whole house from top to bottom, but the amount we did find was small. I do not remember the precise amount we got, but it did not exceed two hundred dollars, and to our great displeasure we afterwards found out, that there was a large amount of gold and silver in the house at the time, that we did not find.

After we had plundered the house to our satisfaction, of all the money we could find, and each one of us had his load of the most valuable articles about, we set the house on fire and burnt everything up, together as we thought with Mrs. Maffitt who we thought was dead, and we left with a full conviction in our own minds that she would be burnt in the house. When I afterwards learned that she was not dead, I often wondered at her providential escape.

The gold and silver we had overlooked, was all melted, and I understood that Maffitt afterwards took it to Mobile and disposed of it.

Wages, in his adventure, was not so successful as we were. On the same night, he and McIntosh camped near Tallahala, not far from old Sumrall's and in the vicinity of Bryant Barlow's. Barlow happened to pass their camp early in the night and discovered Wages. He raised a company and got after

C—7

Wages, themselves and dogs, and Wages had to leave and take the woods for home again. McIntosh and Wages' wife turned back for Mobile on the Big Creek place, where they all landed about five days after. There we were all in the vicinity of Mobile again; Wages had made a water haul and we had done worse. Wages was laying out, Brown and myself were in the same situation. It became necessary for Wages, McGrath and I to hold a private consultation, relative to our future operations, and to devise some plan to get rid of old Brown. We could see no way to do that, unless it would be to lie to him and frighten him to leave, which we did. Our next plan was to manage to get our money from Catahoula, and deposit it about the Bay of St. Louis, near the sea coast, where we could get it on a boat. Wages and McGrath were to attend to that matter, and I was to assist Brown over the Mississippi. So wages went to Brown and told him that there was a reward for both of them, and said he, "I am going to leave, and you had better do the same, for Maflitt has a crowd now on the look out for us." Brown had but little money. He then enjoined it upon Wages to take Harvey's note and give him the money for it. Said he, "if he won't pay the note you and McGrath kill the d——d rascal." So saying, Wages gave him the money for the note, and loaned him sixty dollars more, and then told Brown that James Copeland would go with him and assist his family to travel, while he, Brown, could dodge before and behind. So the matter was understood, and in a few nights Brown rolled off and crossed Dog River at Ward's bridge, where Wages, McGrath and I joined him; I took charge of the teams and family, and Brown took his rifle and to the woods, mostly in the day-time. We did not want for fresh meat; Wages and McGrath left for Catahoula by way of Harvey's, and crossed at Fairley's; we crossed at Robert's and old Green court house, and up Black Creek, on by Columbia, Holmesville and so on to the mouth of Red River. After crossing the Mississippi, I loaned old Brown twenty-five dollars more, bid him good-by and returned to the vicinity of Mobile. I was gone over four weeks.

## WAGES AND M'GRATH KILLED BY HARVEY.

On my way back I learned at Black Creek, of the death of Wages and McGrath. They had got into some difficulty with Harvey about the forty dollar note, and he shot and killed them both. This news sounded in my ears like thunder; and so astounded was I that I lost for the time all my senses. However, after a little reflection, I began to think over my situation, and a thousand thoughts hurled through my brain. Almost instantly, it seemed that every crime I had ever committed in my life was then pictured before my eyes and the awful consequences attending them. The object, for which I committed them, was money; and it was now doubtful whether I should ever obtain that, or not. Upon further reflection, I recollected that Wages had given me a diagram or map of the place where our, now my money was hidden, and a direction of the course so that I certainly could find it. Stimulated with the idea of being worth thirty thousand dollars, I began to cheer up and returned home.

## REWARD OF ONE THOUSAND DOLLARS OFFERED FOR HARVEY'S SCALP.

The first thing was to procure my map or diagram, which I did. I found all my friends grieving. The first word asked me by old man Wages and the old lady was: "What are you going to do, James? Are you not going to seek vengeance on that Harvey?" Both then said to me, "James we will give you one thousand dollars for Harvey's scalp, if you will kill the rascal or have it done." I then told them I would see some of my friends, and let them know in a short time.

A short time after that I received a notice to attend a meeting of the clan, at our Wigwam in the city, on a certain night. So I disguised myself and went into the city and attended, and in that meeting I met several officers of the city, such as constables, deputy sheriff, etc., who all told me not to be afraid;

that there would be no exertion to arrest me. There were a number of resolutions passed commemorative of the demise of our departed friends and brothers Gale H. Wages and Charles McGrath. After the adoption of these resolutions, I then raised the question before the meeting as to the propriety of taking up with old Wages' offer; and after explaining that offer to the meeting, it was unanimously approved; and I was nominated to head and lead the band on that expedition, with power to select as many, and just such men of our clan as I thought necessary. So I selected Jackson Pool, Sam. Stoughton, John Copeland and Thomas Copeland. I selected them because they were good woodsmen, and I knew that Pool and Stoughton were brave.

After I had made the selection, I called them all together and we held a consultation. It was agreed that we would go and make the trial on Harvey; but that we must have five hundred dollars from old Wages in advance. I went to old Wages, and told him what was our conclusion. He hesitated at first, and offered to give us security that the money should be paid when we had done the job; I told him, "no! it was a dangerous undertaking, and we must be paid something to start with." Finally, after consulting with his wife, he agreed to give us the five hundred dollars. Our only business then was to prepare ourselves with the best of double-barrell guns and pistols and bowie knives, with plenty of ammunition and percussion caps of the best quality, and thus armed and equipped we were ready for our journey.

Now I had a two fold object in view; that was, to go on to Catahoula, and search for my money, and for that purpose I took with me my diagram or map. The old man forked over the five hundred dollars, and we made ready for the start.

On Sunday morning the 8th day of July, 1858, we all set out from Wages' place on Big Creek, where we had assembled for that purpose. We had not traveled far' before Thomas Copeland was taken sick and turned back, at Dog River. We then traveled on by Fairley's ferry, the O'Neal settlement and by James Batson's to Harvey's place. We traveled leisurely and camped out every night. We did not stop at any house after we left Pascagoula, and we reached Harvey's place early in the day on the Saturday following. I was well acquainted with the place for I had been there with Wages and McGrath when Allen Brown lived there.

We found the house empty, but from appearances we judged that the farm was cultivated. We saw signs of foot steps about the house and yard, from which we inferred that Harvey was in the habit of coming about there daily. Our next business was to prepare for action. We went into the house and made many port holes on every side, so that we could shoot Harvey, let him approach which ever side he would. Our next business was to examine around the premises for his path, and place a sentinel there in ambush for his arrival. This sentinel was cautiously relieved every two or three hours, whilst the balance of us remained close inside or about the house, eating figs, peaches and water melons and destroying more than we eat.

In the afternoon we began to get hungry; I proposed to the balance to go over to Daniel Brown's, about a mile and get some bread and meat for us all. Pool and Stoughton objected, and said, "there is plenty of green corn in the field; let us make a fire and roast some of the ears and eat here." I then objected, and told them that if Harvey discovered a smoke in the house he would take the hint, and give the alarm, and that we should have the whole of Black and Red Creek down upon us. They still persisted, and Stoughton went into the field, gathered about twenty ears of the best and greenest corn and brought them into the house. Pool went out and brought in a load of wood and made a large fire and they roasted their corn.

That was precisely what betrayed us—the smoke issuing from the chimney of the house.

After the corn was roasted, we all eat heartily; John Copeland was on guard ; Pool took his place, and John came in and eat. A little before sunset it was Stoughton's time to relieve Pool. My brother John proposed to Stoughton to let him relieve Pool, and for Stoughton to take the next watch around the house. So it was agreed, and Pool came to the house.

## PRESENTIMENT OF POOL'S DEATH.

Awhile after sunset, Stoughton, Pool and I were sitting on the gallery, talking very low, about the way we should have to manage. We were fearful Harvey was not at home, or had left the country. Some of us were eating figs and some eating peaches. All of a sudden our attention was arrested by a large white fowl, which passed through the yard some fifteen or twenty yards from us. It was a kind of fowl that I had never seen before, nor had either of my comrades, as they asserted. It walked some ten or fifteen yards; we rose to get a more minute view, and it took flight and ascended, until we lost sight of it in the distance. This seemed to strike Pool with terror and amazement, and he reflected a few minutes and said, "Boys, I shall be a dead man before to-morrow night! That is an omen of my death!"

Stoughton laughed and said to Pool, that if he was a dead man he would make a very noisy corpse ; but Pool still insisted that it was a signal of his death, and urged hard that we should leave that place, and retire to one more secluded. "I did wrong," said he, "in making fire in the house." We tried to laugh him out of his predictions, but all to no purpose ; and sure enough, as he had conjectured, before the next night he was a corpse.

Just before dark, Stoughton went to where brother John was stationed, and they both remained until after dark ; they then came up to the house, and Stoughton mounted guard. All this time Pool appeared to be in a deep study and had nothing to say, appeared dejected and low spirited. We all laid down,

THE FAMOUS HARVEY BATTLE.—[See page 103.

except Stoughton, to try to sleep; I could see Pool and John; they could not sleep. The moon rose two or three hours before day, and I got into a doze several times and each time the most huge serpents would be after me, that I ever beheld. This would waken me, and finally I got up and walked about; I found Pool was up. Stoughton said he could not sleep, and brother John got up and said he could not sleep. We then consulted together and Pool was for leaving the place before day. Stoughton objected, and said, "Let's wait until eight or nine o'clock in the morning; after Harvey gets his breakfast he may come to the orchard for fruit. If he does not come by this time, we may leave."

Daylight made its appearance not long after that, and shortly after the sun 'rose, and poor Pool said after the sun had risen above the horizon: "How beautiful the sun looks this morning; the sky looks so pure, clear and serene!" Poor fellow! it was the last sun that he ever beheld encircling this earth.

### THE FAMOUS HARVEY BATTLE.

The time passed on until between eight or nine o'clock. We were all out in the yard, eating figs and peaches; John Copeland all at once cried out: "Boys, there comes a young army of Black Creek men!" We all dodged into the house. Pool seized his gun, and says, "boys take your guns!" I said to him, "they will not trouble us; they are a company out hunting, and are coming in here for figs and water melons and other fruit; they are not in pursuit of us!" "Yes they are," said Pool, "and I will sell my life as dear as I can!" So saying he cocked both barrels of his gun and pistol and eased his bowie knife in the sheath.

We had given no instructions, only to be silent and remain still. They seemed to separate and go in different directions. On coming near the house, some one of their company hailed to the balance, "come on, boys, here they are!" "There!"

said Pool, "I told you so." So soon as we heard this, we knew that we had been discovered, and that it was to kill or be killed.

I made my escape out of the house the first opportunity I saw, dodged around a big fig tree, and looked back a moment at the house. Pool was standing in the door with his gun at a poise. Harvey came round the corner of the house, on Pool's right, and jumped into the gallery; Pool immediately fired, and struck Harvey in the left side. Harvey immediately squared himself and shot the contents of his whole load in Pool's side, and fell on the gallery. Pool stepped into the yard, and another man shot him in the breast, and he immediately fell dead.

At this moment Stroughton and John Copeland jumped out of the door and ran; I wheeled immediately as the crowd rushed around the house, and ran. At the report of the next gun, the shot whistled all around my head, I then heard several guns. It appeared to me there must have been five hundred at that moment; and I have no doubt that I made the best running there that I ever made in my life before. In fact, it seemed to me that it was no trouble, that I never touched the ground, but flew over it.

After I had got a sufficient distance from the place, and found I was not pursued by any of their party, I stopped to reflect to myself, and wondered what had become of Stoughton and my bother John. Pool, I knew, must be dead, for I saw him fall, and the blood gush from the wound. I felt almost certain that Stoughton and my brother John were both killed also, from the number of guns I heard fired, as I thought.

It was then that I more seriously meditated on my situation than I ever had done before, and wondered to myself what I should do for the best. I felt very sad, and thanked my God for my providential escape, believing that all the rest of my comrades were in eternity. But after I had thus meditated and reflected upon the past, I felt that I deserved death, when all my crimes again stared me full in the face. I then formed a stern resolution within my own breast, that if God would permit me ever again to reach my home, that I would refrain from all my evil ways, and become a Christian, believing that God had been merciful to me, in preserving me, and hurling my comrades and associates into another world.

After a while I became more collected and concluded I would go over to Daniel Brown's, who, I knew, did not live far from that place. I had been there but a short time when my brother John came up, bare-headed, and mud above his knees, where he had run through a muddy reed-brake. He called me to one side, and in a few words he told me that Stoughton was not killed, but Pool was, and that our enemies had left there. He saw them carrying Harvey away, and he thought Harvey was dead; that we had better go over and do something with Pool and get Stoughton, and leave.

This was on Sunday, the 15th of July, 1848. Several persons had accidently happened in at Brown's that day. I went into the house and told the company what had happened over to the other house, since I left; that there had been some shooting done, and that Pool was killed, and I expected Harvey was; that we were on our way to Honey Island, and stopped there for the night; and that I had come over to Brown's to get some bread baked, and that it had all occurred since I left; and that I would like to go over and do something with Pool, and see if Stoughton was killed. A number of persons went with us to the place, some ladies among the rest. When we got there we found Pool lying dead. We laid him straight on his back. I recollected that he had some money, and I soon sounded his pockets, and obtained one hundred and twenty dollars of the money I had given him. There was a five dollar gold piece missing. I took all he had. As he had other means, I knew that the money would do him no good then. I went into the house and got John Copeland's hat, and went down to the side of the swamp and called

Stoughton, and he came out. We were then all together again, except Pool.

We gathered our guns, returned to Brown's, eat dinner, and left for home. But in the affray I had lost my memorandum book, and in that book was the diagram or map and directions where to find the money which belonged to Wages, McGrath and myself; I hunted for it diligently, but could not find it. It certainly went in a very mysterious way, and I have often since thought that the decree of Justice forbid me enjoying that money.

After we left Brown's that day, we traveled on the same route we had come. We slept in the woods that night, and next day we got something to eat at Peter Fairley's, and so continued our journey on home, where we arrived on Sunday, the 22d of July, having been gone just fourteen days. When we arrived, old Wages was highly pleased that Harvey was killed, and he and the old lady very promptly settled with us. He paid us off with his place on Big Creek, in part, and the balance in hogs, cattle, pony horses, carts and farming tools and utensils. My father and mother, with the family, removed to the place.

In a very little while after that, the times began to be very squally. Old Wages and his wife had to pull up stakes, take their negroes and leave the country, at a great sacrifice of their property. I was already an outlaw; my brother John now became one with me. Stoughton, like a fool, as he was, took a yoke of oxen, or some cattle, which he had received from Wages in part pay for his services, to Mobile for sale. While there, he was arrested and put in jail, under the requisition of the Governor of Mississippi, and conveyed from Mobile to Perry county, where he was tried and convicted twice. The first conviction was reversed by the Appellate Court, and while in prison, waiting a second hearing, he died. So went another of our clan to eternity.

I still continued laying out and hiding myself from place to place, fully intending to leave the country just as soon as I could settle my business; and I even made several appointments of times that I would go, but some way, or somehow, there appeared to be a supernatural power which controlled my every action, and I could not leave the vicinity of Mobile.

During that fall and winter my brother John and I made two trips from Big Creek to Catahoula to hunt for that money, and the last trip we made I was prepared to leave. Brother John had left the principal part of his money at home, and had to go back after it, and he prevailed on me to go with him. We returned to the vicinity of Mobile, where I loitered away my time for some month or two, and it seemed that my mind in some way became confused and impaired, and I took to drinking too much spiritous liquors. One day, some time in the spring of 1849, my brothers John, Thomas, Isham or Whinn, and I were at a little grocery store near Dog river, about twelve miles from Mobile. I drank too much spirits and became intoxicated, and in that situation I imagined every man I saw was trying to arrest me. I fell in with a man by the name of Smith, an Irishman, and a difficulty occurred between us; I concluded that he intended to arrest me. I drew my double-barrel shot gun upon him and intended to kill him. He was too quick for me; he threw up my gun, drew his dirk and stabbed me just above the collar bone. The wound did not quite penetrate the cavity of the chest, or it would have killed me; I threw down my gun and ran about two hundred yards and fainted. My brothers then carried me about two miles, and one of them went home and got a carriage and took me home. Smith went to Mobile and told the news. A party came out and tracked me up by the blood, and arrested and carried me to Mobile jail.

I was now in the worst situation I ever was in in my life. One indictment against me in Alabama for larceny, and another against me in Mississippi for murder, and the requisition of the Governor of Mississippi then in the hands of the officer to carry me there to be tried. The question was which trial to avoid; if found guilty, as I felt certain I would be, in both cases, one would be the penitentiary for not less than four years, and the other would be hanging. I employed the best counsel that could be procured in Mobile, and on consulting with him and making him fully acquainted with all the facts, he advised me to plead guilty of the larceny and go to the penitentiary of Alabama; "for," said he, "you may stand some chance after your four years are out to make your escape from the clutches of the law in Mississippi. They may not think to file their requisition with the Governor of Alabama in time, and in that event, when your time expires, you will be let loose."

My trial came on before my wound was near well, and I was brought into court and arraigned, and the indictment read to me in open court. When asked "are you guilty or not guilty?" I plead guilty, after which my counsel addressed the court and prayed its indulgence in passing sentence, and that the term of punishment be made as short as the law would permit, which was accordingly done, and sentence of four years at hard labor in the penitentiary of Alabama was passed upon me.

I accordingly served out my four years at Wetumpka, Ala., and all to avoid going to Mississippi to be tried for the murder of Harvey.

However, I did not evade the rigor of the laws of Mississippi. The vigilance of the Sheriff of Perry county threw a guard around me, that secured to him the possession of my person at the expiration of my time in the penitentiary of Alabama, and he immediately transferred me to the county jail of Perry county, Mississippi.

I remained in the jail of Perry and Covington counties upward of two years before I had a trial. I was found guilty of murder; and the sentence of death was passed upon me, and the day appointed for my execution. Within eight days of the time the Sheriff informed me that my time was only eight days, and that my rope, shroud and burial clothes were all ready. He then read to me the death warrant! My tongue nor pen cannot express my feelings on that occasion during that day and night. However, to my great joy, the next morning he brought me the glorious news that the clerk of the court had received a supersedeas and order to respite my execution, and carry my case to the High Court of Errors and Appeals.

I cannot express my joyful feelings on receiving this intelligence. It removed that cloud of horror and despair, which was lowering upon and around me, and renovated anew my whole soul. It was to me as a refulgent light from the sun of heaven cast upon the dark and gloomy vale; but, alas, how ephemeral that sunshine of joy and bliss! That fickle dame, Fortune, upon whose wheel I had so successfully floated in former days, finally brought me to the same point where I started.

I was, therefore, conveyed from the Perry county jail to the State penitentiary at Jackson, to await there a hearing of my case in the High Court of Errors and Appeals, and remained there about two years. In the meanwhile my case was argued before this Court, and the judgment reversed, and the cause remanded for further proceedings in the Circuit Court of Perry county.

# TRIAL OF JAMES COPELAND.

### TRANSCRIPT OF THE JUDICIAL PROCEEDINGS.

At the September term of said Court, in the year A. D. 1857, on Wednesday of the term, it being the 16th day of the month, James Copeland was taken to the Bar of the Court and arraigned upon an indictment, found by the following Grand Jury at the March term, 1857, to-wit: John McCallum, Lemuel Strahan, John W. Carter, Allen Travis, Lewis H. Watts, James Chappell, G. W. Rawls, Wm. Jenkins, Peter McDonald, Malachi Odom, Joseph G. Young, James M. Bradler, Sr., Stephen Smith, Wm. Hinton, Edmund Merritt, Sidney Hinton, Joseph T. Breeland, Henry Dearman, Lorenzo Batson and John Fairley, Foreman—which indictment was as follows:

STATE OF MISSISSIPPI,  }
PERRY COUNTY.           }

*In the Circuit Court of Perry County—At March Term*, 1857.

The Grand Jurors for the State of Mississippi, summoned, empanneled, sworn, and charged to inquire in and for the State of Mississippi, and in and for the body of the county of Perry, upon their oath, present, that James Copeland, late of said county, on the 15th day of July, Anno Domini, one thousand eight hundred and fifty-eight, with force and arms in the county of Perry aforesaid, in upon one James A. Harvey, then and there being in the peace of God and the said State of Mississippi, feloniously, wilfully and of his malice aforethought.

did make an assault; and that the said James Copeland, a certain shot gun, then and there loaded and charged with gun powder and divers leaden shot, which shot gun, so loaded and charged he, the said James Copeland, in both his hands, then and there, had and held, to, at, against and upon the said James A. Harvey, then and there feloniously, wilfully and of the malice aforethought of him, the said James Copeland, did shoot off, and discharge; and that the said James Copeland, with the leaden aforesaid, out of the shot gun aforesaid, then and there by force of the gun powder, shot and sent forth as aforesaid, the said James A. Harvey, in and upon the left side of him the said James A. Harvey, then and there feloniously, wilfully and of the malice aforethought of him, the said James Copeland, did strike, penetrate and wound, giving to the said James A. Harvey, then and there, with the leaden shot so as aforesaid, discharged and sent forth, out of the shot gun aforesaid, by the said James Copeland, in and upon the left side of him, the said James A. Harvey, a little below the left shoulder of him the said James A. Harvey, divers mortal wounds of the depth of three inches, and of the breadth of one quarter of an inch, of which the said mortal wounds, the said James A. Harvey, from the fifteenth day of July in the year aforesaid, until the twenty fifth day of July in the year aforesaid, languished, and languishing did live; on which said twenty-fifth day of July in the year aforesaid, the said James A. Harvey in the county of Perry aforesaid, of the mortal wounds aforesaid, died; and the jurors aforesaid, upon their oaths aforesaid, do further present, that John Copeland, late of the county aforesaid, on the day and year first aforesaid, in the county of Perry aforesaid, feloniously, wilfully and of his malice aforethought, was present, aiding, abetting and assisting the said James Copeland the felony and murder aforesaid to do and commit; and the jurors aforesaid upon their oath aforesaid do say, that the said James Copeland and John Copeland him the said James A. Harvey, in manner and form aforesaid, feloniously,

wilfully and of their malice aforethought did kill and murder,
against the peace and dignity of the State of Mississippi.

GEORGE WOOD, *District Attorney.*

Upon this indictment was indorsed "A true bill signed, John
Fairley, foreman."

At the September Term the following proceedings were had
in the case: "Be it remembered that there was begun and held
a regular Term of the Circuit Court in and for the county of
Perry and State of Mississippi, at the Court House of said
county, in the town of Augusta, the place designated by law
for holding said court, on the second Monday of September, in
the year of our Lord one thousand eight hundred and fifty-
seven, it being the 14th day of said month, present the Hon.
W. M. Hancock, presiding Judge of the 8th Judicial District
of Mississippi, George Wood, Esq., District Attorney for the
said 8th Judicial District, James R. S. Pitts, Sheriff of Perry
county and James Carpenter, Clerk of said Court.

STATE OF MISSISSIPPI,
    *vs.*                    } MURDER.
JAMES COPELAND.

This day comes George Wood, District Attorney, who prosecutes for the State of Mississippi, and the prisoner is brought
to the bar in custody of the Sheriff, and upon notice of the
District Attorney, a special venue for thirty-six free holders, or
house holders, of Perry county, and liable to jury service
therein, ordered returnable to-morrow morning, at 8 o'clock;
the prisoner, in his own proper person, waiving two days'
service of a list thereof and a copy of the indictment, consent-
ing that it be returned at said time; and upon suggestion that
the prisoner is insane, it is ordered that the Sheriff of Perry
county summons twelve good and lawful men of said county,
to be and appear before said Court on Tuesday morning at 8
o'clock A. M., to take inquisition as to the case of lunacy, and
try whether the prisoner be of sound mind and understanding.

TUESDAY MORNING, 8 O'CLOCK.

Court met pursuant to adjournment. Present as on yesterday.

STATE OF MISSISSIPPI }
      *vs.*        } MURDER.
JAMES COPELAND. }

This day comes George Wood, the District Attorney, who prosecutes for the State of Mississippi, and the prisoner is brought to the bar, in custody of the Sheriff, whereupon comes a jury of good and lawful men, to wit: Porter J. Myers, Malachi Odom, Sr., J. M. Bradley, Jr., Darling Lott, Malcolm McCallum, Angus McSwain, Q. A. Bradley, J. M. Bradley, Sr., Wm. H. Nicols, W. C. Griffin, D. S. Sapp and James Edwards, who are regularly summoned, elected and sworn, and well and truly to try an issue joined, *ore tenus*, whether or not the prisoner be of sound mind, and whether he possesses sufficient intellect to comprehend the cause of the proceedings on the trial, so as to be able to make a proper defense; or whether the appearance of insanity, if any such be proven, is feigned or not; and the evidence having been submitted to them in the presence of the prisoner, they retired to consider of their verdict, and in his presence returned the following, to-wit: "We, the jury, on our oaths, find the prisoner sane; that he possesses sufficient intellect to comprehend the cause of the prosecution on the trial, so as to be able to make a proper defense, and that the appearance of insanity which he has exhibited, is feigned."

And thereupon the prisoner is arraigned on the charge of murder, as preferred by the bill of indictment; and upon said arraignment, says that he is not guilty in manner and form as therein and thereby charged, and for the truth of said plea he puts himself upon the country; and the District Attorney in behalf of the State of Mississippi doeth the like.

And thereon come the following good and lawful men of Perry county, to-wit: Zebulon Hollingsworth, J. J. Bradley, John A. Carnes, Francis A. Allen, Wm. W. Dunn, Adam Laird, who were regularly summoned on the special venue returned in this case, and who in the presence of the prisoner are regularly tried and chosen between the prisoner and the State; and the special venue being exhausted the Sheriff proceeded to call the regular jurors in attendance at this term, and Daniel S. Sapp, Seaborne Hollingsworth and Francis Martin were in the presence of the prisoner tried, and chosen between the State and the prisoner; and the regular jury being exhausted, the Sheriff is directed to summon thirteen bystanders as jurors, and from the number so summoned as last aforesaid, Milton J. Albritton was in presence of the prisoner duly tried and chosen between the State and the prisoner; and the said thirteen persons so last summoned being exhausted, it is ordered that a venue issue, commanding the Sheriff to summon twenty good and lawful men of Perry county, to be and appear before the court to-morrow morning at 8 o'clock, A. M., to serve as jurors in the trial of the issue aforesaid, and the prisoner is remanded to jail, and John W. Carter is sworn as baliff to take charge of the jury.

---

WEDNESDAY MORNING, 8 OCLOCK, SEPTEMBER 16, 1857.

STATE OF MISSISSIPPI  
    *vs.*    }   MURDER.  
JAMES COPELAND.

This day comes George Wood, District Attorney, and the prisoner is again brought to the bar, in custody of the Sheriff, and also comes the jury whom yesterday were duly tried, chosen and taken between the parties; and thereupon comes James M. Pitts and John H. Holder, who were this day returned as jurors in the case, in obedience to the command of the venue, last issued on yesterday; who in presence of the prisoner are regularly tried, chosen and taken between the parties; and the jury so chosen, as aforesaid, are empaneled and sworn, in the presence of the prisoner, well and truly to try the traverse upon the issue joined between the State and the prisoner aforesaid, and a true deliverance make according to the evidence; and the evidence is submitted to them in the presence of the prisoner, and the opening argument is heard, on the part of the District Attorney, and the further consideration of the cause is continued until to-morrow morning, and the prisoner is remanded to jail.

---

Thursday Morning, 8 o'clock, September 17, 1857.

State of Mississippi  
        vs.       } Murder.  
James Copeland.

This day comes the District Attorney, and the prisoner is again brought to the bar in the custody of the Sheriff, and the argument is resumed and concluded; and the jury are instructed by the Court at the request of the counsel, in writing, and the jury retire to consider their verdict. And in the presence of the prisoner return the following, to-wit: "We, the jury, on our oaths, find the prisoner guilty in manner and form as charged in the bill of indictment;" and the prisoner is remanded to jail to await his sentence.

---

## SENTENCE OF THE COURT.

---

Friday Morning, 8 o'clock, September 18, 1857.

State of Mississippi  
        vs.       } Murder.  
James Copeland.

This day comes the District Attorney, and the prisoner, who was on yesterday convicted of the crime of murder, is again brought to the bar. And thereupon the prisoner by his counsel moves the Court for a new trial, which motion was fully heard and understood by the Court; and is by the Court here overruled. And to the opinion of the Court in overruling said motion, the prisoner by his counsel here excepts:

STATE VS. JAMES COPELAND. } MURDER.
MOTION FOR NEW TRIAL OF THE COLLATERAL.

Issue joined as to the sanity of the defendant, and his capacity to make defense in the charge of murder.

1st. Because the Court erred in refusing instructions asked by defendant and in granting those asked by the State.

2d. Because said verdict is contrary to law and evidence.

TAYLOR & WILBORN, for Motion.

And the prisoner being asked what further he had to say why the sentence of death should not be passed upon him, says nothing in bar or preclusion. "It is therefore considered by the Court, here, and is so ordered and decreed, that the prisoner be taken hence to the jail from whence he came, and there safely kept until the thirtieth day of October, in the year of our Lord one thousand eight hundred and fifty-seven; and that the Sheriff take him thence on the said day, between the hours of ten o'clock in the forenoon and four o'clock in the afternoon of said day, to the place appointed by law, for execution; and that he, the said James Copeland, on the said day, between the hours aforesaid, be hung by the neck until he be dead."

# THE DEATH WARRANT.

THE STATE OF MISSISSIPPI,
To the Sheriff of Perry County—*Greeting:*

Whereas, at the September term, A. D. 1857, of the Circuit Court of said county, on the fourth day of said term, James Copeland was duly convicted of the murder of James A. Harvey, by a verdict of a Jury chosen and sworn between the parties; and whereas, on Friday, the fifth day of said term, by the order and decree of said Court, the said Copeland was sentenced to be hung by the neck until he be dead, on the thirtieth day of October, in the year of our Lord one thousand eight hundred and fifty seven, between the hours of ten o'clock, A. M., and four o'clock, P. M., at the place appointed by law.

These are therefore to command you, in the name, and by the authority of the State of Mississippi, to take the body of the said James Copeland, and him commit to the jail of said county, and him there safely keep, until the said thirtieth day of October, and that on the said thirtieth day of October, between the hours of ten o'clock, A. M., and four o'clock, P. M., of said day, at the place appointed by law, you hang him by the neck until he be dead, dead, dead.

Given under my hand and seal, this, the 18th day of September, A. D. 1857.

[Seal.]                           W. M. HANCOCK, *Judge*.

# THE EXECUTION.

The day arose clear and beautiful on which the sentence of the law and of outraged humanity was to be executed on the man who had so often violated their most sacred behests. The sky was blue and serene; the atmosphere genial; all nature was calm and peaceful; man alone was agitated by the various strong emotions which the execution of the fatal sentence of retributive justice on a fellow-man could not but create.

The place of execution was distant from the city of Augusta one-quarter of a mile. The gallows was erected on a beautiful elevation that was surrounded by the verdure of shrubby oak and the tall, long-leaf pine. The ground was everywhere occupied by thousands of spectators, gathered from Perry and the surrounding counties, to witness the solemn scene. It was indeed one that they will long remember.

About the hour of noon, the prisoner, after being neatly clad, was led from the jail by the officers of the law, placed in the ranks of the guard formed for the occasion, and the procession moved slowly toward the fatal spot.

Soon the doomed man appeared on the gallows. The death warrant was then read to him, and he was informed that he had but a short time to live.

He proceeded to address the awe-struck and silent multitude. He especially urged the young men present to take warning from his career and fate, and to avoid bad company. His misfortune he attributed principally to having been misled while young.

When he had concluded, a number of questions were asked by the immediate spectators, in relation to crimes which had

EXECUTION OF JAMES COPELAND.—[See Page 118.

transpired within their knowledge; but he would give no direct answer—shrewdly eluding the inquiries.

The Sheriff then asked him, in hearing of many lookers-on, if the details of his confession, previously made to that officer, were true. He replied that they were.

His hands were then tied and the cap pulled over his face, and he was told that he had but a few moments to live. He exclaimed, "Lord, have mercy on me!" and he was praying when the drop fell, and a brief struggle ended his blood-stained career.

## GRAND JURY.

John McCullum,
Lemuel Strahan,
John W. Carter,
Allen Travis,
Lewis H. Watts,
James Chappell,
G. W. Rawls,

Wm. Jenkins,
Peter McDonald,
Malachi Odom,
Joseph G. Young,
Jas. M. Bradley, Sr.,
Stephen Smith,
Wm. Hinton,

Edmund Merritt,
Sidney Hinton,
Jos. T. Breeland,
Henry Dearman,
Lorenzo Batson,
John Fairley,
*Foreman.*

## WITNESSES.

Wm. Johnson,
Chancey B. Stevens,
Wm. Landman,
Gibson Waley,
John Anderson,
Wm. C Griffin,
Moses Fullingam,

Laoma Batson,
Jas. Batson,
David Dubusk, Sr.,
Jefferson Williams,
David Dubusk, Jr.,
Wm. Griffin,
Peter Fairley, Sr.,

Peter Fairley, Jr.,
Alexander Fairley,
Sampson Spikes,
Westley Spikes,
W. H. Nicols,
John Fairley,
*Prosecutor.*

## MEMBERS OF THE COPELAND AND WAGES CLAN.

| | | |
|---|---|---|
| J. Baker, | S. S. Shoemake, | A. Brown, |
| C. W. Moore, | J. Gillet, | D. Brown, |
| W. W. Ratlief, | W. Brown, | N. McIntosh, |
| G. Buskings, | J. Taylor, | E. Myrick, |
| J. Harper, | S. Teapark, | J. F. Wright, |
| J. Bowings, | J. Pool, | J. Dewit, |
| J. W. Westly, | John Copeland, | W. Ross, |
| J. Whitfield, | T. Copeland, | W. Sanferd, |
| J. Whitlom, | Henry Copeland, | J. McClain, |
| J. Porter, | Wm. Copeland, | S. Harden, |
| J. Butler, | J. Elva, | J. Harden, |
| J. Hopkins, | H. Sanford, | J. Waters, Jr., |
| J. Harper, | R. Cable, | G. Clealand, |
| W. P. Hobs, | J. Hevard, | — Moulton, |
| W. C. Whelps, | G. Daniels, | — Overall, |
| Jasper Whitlow, | G. H. Wages, | G. Young, |
| E. Sharper, | C. H. McGraffin, | Thos. Hix, |
| T. Powell, | Chas. McGrath, | J. Alfred, |
| J. Doty, | J. Welter, | J. Kelly, |
| D. Doty, | G. Welter, | A. Watson. |

NOTE.— If the guilty should not, by any means be screened, yet if positive doubts exist, the suspected should have the benefit of such doubts. Accordingly the initials to the names of Moulton and Overall have been omitted; as the jury on "trial" expressed doubts as to what particular parties Copeland referred to in the names given. There are many by the same name, and even part of the same initials, yet have no affinity in anything else. It is said that "public sentiment is seldom wrong, and never wrong long;" therefore with all the circumstances before it, it is requested that the public will approach the subject with an unprejudiced mind, and decide faithfully and justly to all parties concerned.

# LETTER OF JAMES COPELAND TO HIS MOTHER.

(*Written the night before his Execution.*)

AUGUSTA, MISSISSIPPI, October 29th, 1857.

MRS. REBECCA COPELAND:

*My dear Mother* — It is with painful feelings indeed, that I attempt writing to you on the present occasion. I take this opportunity, knowing at the same time, that it is the last one of the kind which I shall ever be permitted to enjoy while here on earth. It is long and much that I have suffered while in prison since my first confinement in Mobile county, and yet it seems as though nothing will pay the debt but my life. I have had my trial and was convicted upon a charge of murder, and I have received the awful sentence of death. The sheriff told me to day, that to morrow at 2 o'clock I will be hanged, according to the order of court. Oh, my dear mother, what an awful sound is this to reach your ear. Oh, would it could be otherwise; but you are aware that I justly merit the sentence. You are knowing to my being a bad man; and dear mother, had you given me the proper advice when young, I would now perhaps be doing well. It is often I have meditated on this subject since my confinement in prison, and often have I recollected my good old father's advice when I was young, and repented a thousand times over, with sorrow and regret, that I have failed to receive it as good, benevolent advice. If such a course I had taken, I have no doubt, but what I would be doing well at this time. But it is too late now to talk of things past and gone. The time has come when I shall have to take my departure from this world, and it pains my heart, to know that I have to leave you and my brothers and sisters; and much am I mortified to think how distantly you have treated me while here in prison. Not the first time have you been to see me; but I can freely excuse you for all this, and I do hope you will prepare to meet Jesus in Heaven.

Dear Mother, long has the time been that life was not any

satisfaction to me. I am now in the dungeon with the cold and icy bands clasped around me, and cold as clay. Much have I suffered, but after two o'clock to-morrow, my troubles will all be over, or worse than they are at present. This I am not able to tell. I have been preparing to meet my God, praying diligently for mercy and for the pardon of my sins, but I do not know whether my prayers have been heard or not.— The Scriptures say "that the spirit of the Lord shall not always strive with man," and again say: "he that calls upon the Lord in the last hours shall be saved." If so, I feel some spark of hope, but I tell you this hope is hanging upon a slender thread.

Dear Mother, it makes the tears trickle down my cold cheeks to have to pen this statement to you. Dear Mother, I have to close this letter. My heart is overflowed already, so when you receive this, you can keep it as a memorial, and remember that poor Jim is no more on earth; that he has bid you a long farewell.

Dear Mother, it appears as though my heart will break at the very thought of this. Oh, could I but see you once more before my death, it would give my aching heart some relief; but we have to part without this pleasure.

Now my good old Mother, I bid you a long farewell, forever and forever.

JAMES COPELAND.

## MYSTIC ALPHABET

Used by the Copeland and Wages Clan, in their secret correspondence and documents.

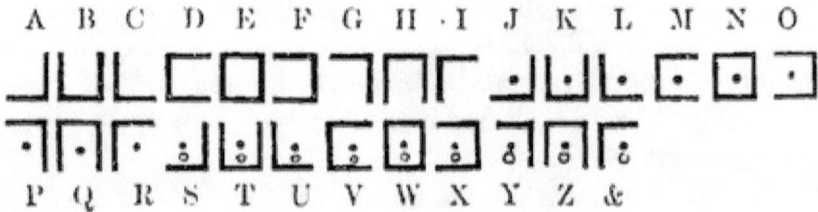

# APPENDIX.

## PLANS DEVISED TO PRESERVE THE LIFE OF COPELAND.

THE LAST BOLD EFFORTS TO SAVE THE LIFE OF JAMES COPELAND PROVED INEFFECTUAL; BUT THE SAME AGENTS SUCCEEDED BY REFINED MOVEMENTS IN PROCURING THE ACQUITTAL OF JOHN COPELAND.

The organization of the Wages and Copeland Clan embraced a diversified talent of an extraordinary grade in different departments of operations. It commanded some of the ablest ability belonging to the bar and the medical profession, with other agents who could be hired or engaged for temporary assistance. It requires more than a cursory contemplation to anything like a full comprehension of the lengths, and breadths, and depths of its vast theaters of operations. Many, perhaps, not admitted to the council and secret conclaves of the organization, could be engaged for a stipulated sum to perform important services in defense and protection of its active members, who might inwardly condemn its pernicious fields of operations against the best interests of society. Whether such conduct can stand the test of reason and argument it is for others, with the reader, to determine. The worse the case the richer the fees for the lawyer, and so of the medical profession. As frequently happens, the lawyer scruples at nothing to win a victory for his client. In some places this course is fashionable and not at all odious. As long as the attorney keeps his defense within legitimate bounds, and avails himself of every lawful opportunity for the advantage of his client, no well-balanced mind can be disposed to censure, because on the other side, the prosecution will do the same. But when foul and corrupt means are resorted to; when the most vicious and depraved of actions are brought in play to screen the guilty and make crime respectable, then it is that public sentiment should be loud against such abominations, no matter whether against the medical or legal profession, or against any other class who can be brought to perform the services of infamy.

The period betwixt the imprisonment and execution of James Copeland, three parties from Alabama came and settled in Perry county, Miss., one in, and the other two about Augusta. These three performed their part so well—so concealed and reserved as to pass for gentlemen in the highest degree respectable. But few, if any, had suspicion until afterward of their object to assist the captured in escaping the last penalties of outraged law.

One of the three, who settled in Augusta; a skilled doctor and surgeon, behaved himself so well in every respect—on all occasions exhibiting a winning and an affable deportment—everybody's friend with the most lavish of generosity—sparing no exertions to gain the confidence and admiration of those in power and of influence; this is the man who proposed to the sheriff the plan to save the life of James Copeland. This proposition was made betwixt the time of his conviction and execution. The particulars are as follows:—The doctor to the sheriff: "There is now a fine opportunity of making one thousand dollars in gold, providing that you will act in concert with me in permitting certain things to be done before the execution of Copeland." There was something so bland, so expert, and so graceful in the conduct of the strange doctor as to make him friends wherever he went. He insinuated himself into the confidence of the sheriff; and when the proposition was made for certain things to be done before execution, for and in consideration of a thousand dollars, the curiosity of the sheriff could not be otherwise than powerfully excited to learn all particulars of the plan in contemplation, and, accordingly, so far indulged or humored the beginning so as to obtain the whole of what was then behind. The doctor continued, and gave the name of him who had a thousand dollars to pay for the preservation of the life of Copeland; and to be done in the following manner, secure from exciting any suspicion whatever. The doctor to the sheriff: "Allow me about half an hour before the time arrives for your taking him out of jail to the place of execution, to go in under the pretence of shaving and dressing him suitably to the solemnity of the occasion, during which time I will perform an operation in tracheotomy by inserting into the trachea, or wind-pipe, a small silver tube sufficient for the admission of air into the lungs to keep up some degree of respiration, so that when he shall have hung the allotted time, he can be cut down and by an extension of the tube, he can be so buried as to prevent the extinction of life; which, as soon as convenient, he can be disinterred and so cared for by artful means until the recovery so far progress as will enable him to successfully escape."

The sheriff listened to all this with a smile, and treated the whole as rather a plausible romance than a possible reality; but firm to the duties of his office, he yielded not to the temptation; yet to maintain good faith as to what transpired before the proposition was fully made, and for prudent considerations in regard to his own safety, he has refrained from publishing this narrative at an earlier date, because conscious that the public interests, though delayed, would best be served by so doing in the long run.

Shortly after the execution of James, John Copeland, the brother of the former, was arrested, brought to the same jail, and tried in the same case, and for the same crime of murder.

The State was represented by George Wood, Esq., and the

defence by Wirt Adams as principal. Both sides labored hard and wonderfully skillful. The argument of the latter occupied about three or four hours in delivery. The evidence against John Copeland was quite as strong as against his convicted brother, but the juries were of different material. The three strange immigrants from Alabama, who then had recently settled in and about Augusta, managed to get on the jury. This was not hard to do, as the county had pretty much been exhausted before to get an acceptable jury not disqualified by some objections brought forth. When the jury retired, the three here referred to, having the most ingenuity, lead the other remaining part, the consequence of which was a verdict of acquittal. This verdict aroused the indignation of the public both far and near—murmurs everywhere, and satisfaction nowhere. So irritated were the populace that, in all probability, the life of Copeland would have been taken by violence the night after his liberation, but for the timely notice given him for immediate escape.

The following morning he was heard from as being seen on the opposite side of Leaf river, about thirty miles below Augusta, in the direction for Pascagoula river. It is supposed he went almost direct to Angelina county, Texas, where his mother and family settled after leaving Mississippi.

But little time had elapsed after this before the Sheriff of Perry received a letter from Col. Pickering, of this (Angelina) county, warning him of the necessity of being on his guard— that Thomas, another brother of the Copeland family, had left that vicinity for Mississippi; and, according to the general belief there, with a design on the life of the Sheriff; but although he passed through the county of Perry, by the way of Black Creek, to Mobile, Alabama, yet if he made any secret movement for the assassination, he never knew it.

The Copeland family, in Angelina county, instituted a formidable prosecution against Col. Pickering, but his reception of the pamphlet containing the confession, caused the District

Attorney of that place to dismiss the prosecution, and for this the Copeland family was heard to swear vengeance against the Sheriff who had published them; therefore, well taken were the grounds of fear entertained by Col. Pickering. Immediately after the acquittal of John Copeland, the three strange immigrants left for parts unknown.

### S. S. SHOEMAKE, THE ARCH-MONSTER OF ATROCITY AND THE PERFECTION OF DECEPTION, WITH HIS JOHN R. GARLAND LETTER.

An organization may soon come to naught, even though founded on principles in every respect sound, healthy and legitimate, if the individuals composing it are defective in brains and energy, the exercise of which are essentially necessary for continued existence. But an organization, based on the contrary of such principles, may continue for years to perpetrate the darkest of human atrocities—spreading terror or devastation both far and wide, if its members, or the leaders, possess the mental force requisite to plan, to command and to execute according to the proper definitions of skill, disguised treachery, and firm intrepidity brought to bear against the less suspecting, but the more honest members of society.

The unfolding of the character of S. S. Shoemake will reveal all the traits of vice, of meanness, of guilt, and of all which contributes to the perfection of human treason and perfidy.

Some of the most masterly strokes of guile and consummate deception are to be found in his John R. Garland letter and the subsequent circumstances with it connected. The ancient Judas fell very far short in comparison with this modern specimen of cruelty, of plunder, and of hypocritical imposture. A marauder, a being destitute of honor, pride or principle, and the very incarnation of all that is vile and abhorent. This is the man whose character, to some extent, will next be unveiled in detail.

But a short time elapsed after the publication of Copeland's confessions until a letter, signed John R. Garland, was received by the Sheriff of Perry county, making inquiry about S. S. Shoemake and two others by the names of J. and D. Doty—all implicated in Copeland's confessions. This letter, as will afterward be shown, was written by Shoemake himself, and was mailed at DeKalb, Kemper county, Mississippi, the substance of which will next be given:

DeKalb, Miss., October —, 1858.
J. R. S. Pitts, Sheriff Perry County, Miss.:

Dear Sir—As I feel very much interested in the future welfare of this immediate section of our country, and am desirous of ascertaining the names of all men of degraded character, so far as practicable, who might chance to live among us, and more especially those characters as represented to you by Copeland, in his recent confessions as a united band of land pirates, which fact has been apparent with me for some years past of the existence of such a clan throughout our entire country. And believing that we have some of the same characters residing within our midst, I thus communicate in confidence to you, trusting that you will be kind enough, on the reception of this, to answer the same, and inform me whether or not the names of S. S. Shoemake, and two other men here, J. Doty and D. Doty, are the same persons as implicated by Copeland in his confessions to you.

So far as the former character is concerned, there is no doubt existing in the minds of the people here but that he belongs to some secret clan. His conduct, and every action through life, go to establish this conclusion. He spends the greater portion of his time away from home, and at times is absent from home for months, none knowing here anything of his whereabouts. And in this way, to the mystery of every one, he makes his peregrinations throughout the country, but whether near or distant is unknown to us. Frequently after having been absent until the community would begin to wonder and ask the question as to the cause of such continued detention, as well as the actuating motives for so much of absence, but none can give any solution—none any intelligence in reference to him. To say the least, there is great suspicion mingled with much curiosity.

Generally when he returns home from making those protracted journeys, he manages so as to arrive some time during the night, bringing with him droves of horses, mules, and sometimes more or less negroes. After his return, the first thing that is known of him, he is seen in the grog-shop bright and early in the morning, waiting the arrival of the bar-keeper for his morning bitters. In this way he seems to be continually whiling away his time—claiming to be acting in behalf of a State committee. On meeting this person, S. S. Shoemake, one that is not personally acquainted with him would not for a moment suspect anything wrong, for he is calculated by his affable deportment, on first acquaintance to make a very favorable impression on the mind.

As we feel much interested in this vicinity relative to this matter, I trust that you will, on receipt of this, give us the desired information above asked for, as there is no favor within your power that you could at this time extend to us that would be received with so much gratitude.

When addressing your communication, you will please remember not to direct to me, but simply address your letter to box, No. 27, DeKalb, Kemper County, Mississippi.

I make the above request in order that my designs may not be frustrated—also, you will please suffer no person to see this communication.

Hoping to hear from you soon, I remain,

Very respectfully,

JOHN R. GARLAND.

This extraordinary letter elicited the following reply:

AUGUSTA, MISSISSIPPI, ———, 1858.

John R. Garland, DeKalb, Miss.:

DEAR SIR—I am in receipt of yours bearing a recent date,

asking me for information relative to certain characters within your vicinity. Giving three names, you wish to know if they are the same persons who were implicated by Copeland in his confession to me.

In answer, at the time of writing the confession, I could have located all the parties given me as members belonging to the Wages and Copeland clan, but did not at the time deem it expedient to do so, because believing that the people in the different sections of the country wherever they might live would be very apt to know them from their general character, But from the description you give of S. S. Shoemake, and from one memorable remark that Copeland made at the time he gave me this name, I am constrained to favor the opinion that he is the same person as both he and yourself have pointed out.

Very respectfully.

J. R. S. PITTS.

---

### SHOEMAKE VISITS THE SHERIFF IN PERSON WITH HIS BOGUS AUTHORITY FROM THE PROBATE JUDGE OF KEMPER COUNTY.

But a short time intervened after the correspondence until Shoemake himself suddenly made his appearance in person at the door of the parlor in which the sheriff at the time was engaged in reading. In reaching so far, Shoemake had passed the outer gate, fronting the street, unnoticed by the watch-dog, or by any of Hon. Drewry Bynum's family with whom the sheriff was boarding. Shoemake boldly opened the parlor door, and, after a graceful and dignified salutation, next inquired if the sheriff was present. Being answered in the affirmative, he was then invited to walk in and take a seat, for which he returned the usual compliments of civility. His next expressed wish was to retire to the sheriff's office, which was situated within a few paces of the dwelling-house—all enclosed within the same yard, as he had communications to make on official business. Both retired accordingly, when, as soon as properly seated, Shoemake drew from his breast pocket a large document, written in a beautiful style and evidently prepared with great care and taste. This instrument of writing was produced to show his authority from the Probate Judge of Kemper county to pursue and apprehend a certain person named and described, for stealing eleven negroes belonging to minor heirs of said county. This instrument of authority was soon detected as counterfeit—not having the legal impress—the court seal of the county from which it pretended to have emanated. This fact, in connection with the introduction of his own name, very properly put the Sheriff on his guard as to subsequent movements which were to follow. Shoemake continued to the effect that the thief, from the direction in which he had been traveling, would be more than likely to cross at the junction of Bowie creek with Leaf river, which is situated about twenty miles above Augusta. Shoemake further added his belief that the thief was making for some point on the seashore at or near Mississippi City, and that he had called on the Sheriff to accompany and assist him in the capture. To this application the Sheriff peremptorily refused, remarking at the same time that the Probate Court was then in session, and that he could not be absent for the period of time necessarily required in a task of this sort without material injury to business transactions and the duties of his office. To this unqualified refusal Shoemake sat for a moment in a silent pause. If the Sheriff himself could not accompany him, he had no desire to have any of the deputies with him.

Appearing very much disappointed in this object to decoy off the Sheriff, and feeling satisfied that all further attempts in this direction would prove abortive, he all at once exhibited a different phase of countenance, and in a jocular manner slapped the Sheriff on the knee, remarking at the same time, "How or where did you get my name associated with the Copeland Clan?" The Sheriff answered, "Why, my dear sir, do you acknowledge the name as recorded in Copeland's confessions as belonging to you?" Shoemake made no direct reply, but observed that the people about where he lived were endeavoring to saddle the reflections on him, and that the same was having a very deleterious effect against him. This being so, he requested of the Sheriff, as an act of favor or kindness, to have his name erased, or disposed of in some other way, such as would remove the odium attached, and that he believed the Sheriff to have the power to do all this with propriety. The Sheriff was a little startled as well as excited at such an absurd proposition, and quickly replied to the following effect: "Your requested favor cannot be performed. The matter has altogether passed out of my hands, and it is utterly beyond my control to make any changes. I have only given publicity to the confessions of Copeland, and if he has wrongfully implicated any one the remedy is by an action of law, or better still, by a counter statement supported by the testimony of those whose veracity cannot be doubted."

Shoemake, discomfitted in his own case on this point, then referred to a correspondence betwixt himself, George A. Cleaveland and others, all of whom were implicated in the pamphlet complained of, and said, from all the information he could gather, unless something was done to relieve the complainants the Sheriff would be sure to have more or less trouble from that quarter. The reply made was pretty much to the same effect as in his own individual case—no hope of success as far as the Sheriff was concerned.

The next question brought forward was an inquiry about a communication from some one at DeKalb, Miss., concerning himself. He was answered in the affirmative to the effect that such a communication had been received. "Very well," said he, "will you be so kind as to let me see it?"

"I cannot," replied the Sheriff, "and for this reason, that the author of it made a special request not to let any person see it; consequently I cannot without a breach of good faith, do violence to the request made and involve myself in difficulties, when all can be so easily avoided." This reply did not satisfy him. He again solicitously pressed for inspection, urging that some d—d rascal had been writing about him, and that he believed it was one by the name of White. He was informed immediately that no person by that name had ever sent any communication whatever, and that he was certainly laboring under wrong impressions in this particular.

He utterly failed to get to see the communication in every effort made for this purpose. The effects were visibly marked on his countenance. Rage and anger, despair and disappointment, with all other of defeated passions, seemed to flit over him in rapid succession; but without any representation in words—only rising with a farewell, such as appeared to the Sheriff ominous of something else, and anything but pleasant in his judgment. After leaving the office he remained in Augusta but a very short time, and when about leaving the place altogether he was heard to say that he would some day meet the Sheriff "at the hatter's shop."

SHOEMAKE RETURNS WITH A WRIT FOR THE SHERIFF'S ARREST.

For some five or six weeks after his departure the Sheriff heard nothing more of him; at the expiration of which time he returned in company with a man by the name of Gilbert, though in reality supposed to be one of the Copeland family. This time he bore a requisition from the Governor of Alabama to the Governor of Mississippi for the body of the Sheriff; and strange, and to this day mysterious as it may appear, the requisition was granted.

Some few days previous to the arrival of Shoemake and his assistant, the Sheriff had left Augusta for the Mississippi Sound on a journey to make arrangements for hymenial considerations. Learning the facts of his absence, they set about gathering all the information they could from negroes and the less suspecting class of others relative to his whereabouts and the anticipated time for his return. Having got the information wanted, forthwith they started in pursuit—traveling the same way by which he was compelled to return to Augusta. It is called the Mississippi Cut Road—better known by the name of the Allsberry and McRae railroad. It runs on range line eight, from Augusta to Mississippi City—all the timber on this line being cut and cleared away some thirty-five years ago. It failed of completion, it is said, through the dishonesty of one or more on whom the responsibility devolved; and the only relic now remaining is a good dirt road, for the benefit of the present traveling community.

On this road, not a great distance from Red Creek, there is an extensive morass, which has been cross-wayed for public accommodation, which otherwise would be impassable on horseback. When Shoemake and his assistant arrived at this place they remained, according to the statements of persons in the neighborhood, one or two days in ambush, stationing themselves one on each side of the cross-way, evidently with a design to prevent the Sheriff from seeing either until he had advanced some distance on it, then to close in upon him from both directions, which would have prevented any earthly chance of escape by any other way—the morass is of such a nature as to swallow up in any other part.

At last becoming impatient, they decided to move on toward the Gulf; and, accordingly, stopped at Red Creek for the night following. But, let it be borne in mind, that they so arranged as to remain at different houses, one on the north, and the other on the south side of the creek, so as to be certain not to miss the Sheriff on his return by that way. The houses where they stopped at for the night were near the ferry—kept for the accommodation of travelers. If the Sheriff had left the coast that morning, as anticipated by the two, he, according to the day's ride, would have been almost certain to have reached one of the houses here referred to, as no other suitable place near could have been found, which would have brought him in direct contact with the pursuers. But by being detained that

AUTHOR MAKING HIS ESCAPE FROM TWO OF THE COPELAND CLAN.—[See Page 135.

morning at Mississippi City, he did not leave in time to reach either place where they were staying, and he of necessity stopped the night in question with an old gentleman by the name of Byrd—about fifteen or twenty miles from the ferry. This old gentleman had been a resident of that section of country for a great number of years, and was well acquainted with Wages and McGrath; also with the truth of many of the incidents as related in Copeland's confessions.

After the usual breakfast hour next morning, the Sheriff availed himself of the earliest opportunity to resume his travel toward Augusta. On his way, some ten or fifteen miles distant from where he that morning started, to his great surprise, he suddenly came in contact with Shoemake and his colleague. They were seated within a one-horse buggy, with another very fine animal fastened to it, and with saddle and other necessaries ready for the rider in case any emergency might occur. They all met together on the top of a little hill, quite steep, with such other circumstances attending as obstructed sight until in quite close contact. The place of meeting was not more than fifty paces from an occupied dwelling house. This fact was, no doubt, the main cause of preventing them from making, perhaps, a fatal attack. The meeting was as of perfect strangers, though, in reality, each side knew the other again. The Sheriff well knew Shoemake, and, from his uneasy countenance, as well as the countenance of the other with him, the Sheriff was satisfied that they knew him.

He having passed, as he thought, a sufficient distance beyond their view, he increased the speed of his horse to a rate of about eight or nine miles an hour for the remainder of the day, which carried him some fifty miles or more from the spot of meeting. He was fully impressed with the idea, at the time of meeting, that they were in pursuit of him for evil and dangerous purposes, which idea was fully confirmed by information gathered that day on travel as to their very suspicious conduct at different points of progress; however, in his heart, he was thankful that he had so far made his escape. His rapid travel onwards for that day was lonely indeed—passing through a wild, desolate region of country, but very sparsely populated—for miles not a human being to be seen; stock in abundance on either side of the road, with here and there frightened deer at seeing him, as it were, flying through space for safety and repose. Night fast coming on, with exhausted fatigue from excessive exercise, and beginning to despair of reaching home that night, he resolved on going to the house of a well-known friend, J. T. Breeland, situated a distance from the highway, and had to be approached with the convenience of a by path. He succeeded in reaching this house in time for late supper. Here he met with all the accommodations that heart could desire. Luxuries plenty, conversation agreeable, with a welcomeness which must ever be appreciated, and more than this, consolation afforded when most needed. The next was retirement for sleep, but little of sound repose was enjoyed; the ghastly scenes of the clan were before his eyes, with struggles for existence betwixt him and his pursuers.

Early next morning, an ample breakfast having been supplied, he, after having received many kindly admonitions from his friend by way of strict caution, left, and reached home, Augusta, about ten o'clock next morning; and about twelve o'clock, only two hours later, Shoemake, with his colleague, also reached the same place.

Immediately on their arrival, he made every preparation for battle, determined to repel force by force if that was their object. But collision was prevented by a timely notice from Hon. Wm. Simmons, to the effect that they had authority from the Governor of Mississippi for his arrest, and that he was at liberty to see the same.

In obedient response to this exhibited authority, Shoemake and his colleague were informed that if they would wait a sufficient length of time to make ready with a number of friends for protection to accompany, he would have no objection whatever to going with them. Their polite answer came to the following effect: "That if desired, they would wait any reasonable length of time to enable him to have all the conveniences wanted."

The news and circumstances connected with his arrest spread throughout the country with almost the speed of electricity. In many instances the reports were very much exaggerated—causing many persons, on the spur of the moment, to become furiously incensed, to such an extent as to threaten the most formidable results of desperation; and but for his appeals for order and due process of law, the most fatal acts of violence might have been committed.

Within a period of three or four days, he had so arranged his business as to be in entire readiness for departure, and so gave notice accordingly. Punctual to the time, he, with about twenty volunteers, mounted and well equipped for protection, when arrangements were made for immediate departure for Mobile, Alabama, all leaving merrily, and soon reached the place of destination. Arriving at the Lafayette House, kept by a Mr. Fulton, in the city of Mobile, all fared while there very sumptuously.

As early as practicable the next morning, the Sheriff went to the office of Hon. Percy Walker, to procure his professional services. This object being accomplished by a compensating fee of five hundred dollars. The next thing to be done was for his counsel to ascertain the amount of the several bonds to be given as required by law. This task was quickly over, the bonds satisfactorily given, and he was immediately released. These last incidents transpired about or near the middle of January, 1859; and the City Court was to open on the 23d of February, following, allowing thirty or forty days to prepare for defence. But before continuing in the connected order, some comments are necessary on what has preceded already.

### SHOEMAKE'S OBJECT WAS ASSASSINATION.

A character so infamously conspicuous as Shoemake's is, should not ordinarily be passed over. It should be thoroughly understood so far as his diabolical conduct is known; and this, in all probability, is only a small part of his treacherous and bloody career. Well might James Copeland remark to the Sheriff in prison: "This said Shoemake is a big dog among us." The foregoing reports of Shoemake's operations are not all; he will again be introduced as playing a distinguished part on the subsequent trial of the Sheriff, and when he will there be pointed out as the main witness for the prosecution, with his oath invalidated, and the worst features of perjury attaching; these, in conjunction with the facts established on trial, sufficiently proved him to be the author of the "John R. Garland letter."

The human machine, as a whole, because of common appearance, does not strike the attention with that force which is essential to a full comprehension of the grand and mighty work produced by an invisible and inscrutable agency of an unseen power. It is dissection, analyzation, and physiological researches which only can reveal the wonderful structure and astounding recovery of the human system. Shoemake's vast fields of diversified operations—mixed, complicated, and clothed in every external form of delusion, when viewed as a whole, but a very imperfect idea can be reached of this covert and monster man. Dissection and analyzation are necessary. The main-springs of his movements must be brought to light. The veils and curtains must be torn away so that the internal workings of his soul can be seen.

Let the reader go back to the time of his writing the John R Garland letter. There will be found a master-peice of dissimulation. Under a fictitious signature, he describes himself, in some particulars of crime and lawlessness, with astonishing accuracy. He gives instructions for the reply to be sent without name to a numbered box in the post office, at DeKalb, under the pretensions of favoring the spread of the printed "confessions" and of dealing heavy blows against Shoemake—the most desperate of human characters.

Some two or three weeks after, this followed by his visit in person to the sheriff of Perry county. Here, suddenly and unexpectedly, he reaches the door of the apartment where the sheriff was seated, unnoticed by the watch dog or by any member of the family. Opens the door and puts on the airs of gentlemanly civility. Pretends to have important official business, so much so as to require secrecy in the sheriff's office. There exhibiting high authority, but feigned and spurious, for capturing a renowned thief, who had succeeded in getting away with eleven negroes; and wants the sheriff to accompany him on such an important expedition over roads wile and desolate. Failing in this object, he next introduces the subject of his own, the John R. Garland letter, and said it had been written by a d———d rascal by the name of White—urging with all his powers of solicitation to see the letter, but without success. He furthermore attempts, by all the arts of sophistry, to induce the sheriff to make changes in the "confessions," and, failing in this, then tries the weapons of intimidation by declaring that trouble more or less must fall on the sheriff if something were not done to relieve George A. Cleaveland and others in Mobile.

The reader perfectly understanding the above, must certainly come to the following conclusion, that Shoemake had a threefold object in view by this visit to the sheriff. First, and the most preferable, was assassination, and, if no opportunity offered for this in his office, to get him off, under false pretensions, on solitary and dreary roads for the better accomplishment of the same. Secondly, to get hold of the John R. Garland letter, which he knew must be very dangerous in any other hands but his own. Thirdly, to publicly kill the sheriff and the "confessions" by inducing him to make changes.

Shoemake when next he appeared in Augusta, it was on a different mission. This time, he was armed with real authority from the Governor of Mississippi for the arrest of the sheriff. But finding him absent, he assiduously and very ingeniously sets to work to gather all possible information as to his whereabouts and the time for his return. This done, in hot pursuit he makes his departure for the seizure of his object. He travels forward with alacrity until he reaches an extensive morass; then, with his colleague, ambushes both sides of it, for a day or two, so as to close in from both ways, if opportunity afforded, on his object, and make escape impossible—ready with a convenient horse for any emergency which might occur. Despairing of meeting with the sought after prize, onward he goes until he reaches the ferry—the distance of a day's ride from Mississippi City, where he expected another opportunity for getting hold of the man he wanted—so arranges as for one to remain on each side of the ferried river—again rendering passage impossible without discovery. Again disappointed, onwards he proceeds, and in a short time comes in contact with the person in pursuit of, but in such a situation as to mar his purposes at that point. They pass, both sides knowing each other. He travels a short distance forward—then turns back after his object, who has fled at the rate of about eight or nine miles the hour—succeeds in reaching Augusta only two hours behind his object. Then makes known his mission of arrest—seeing the tremendous public excitement prevailing which threatened his existence, politely agrees to wait a reasonable length of time for his nominal prisoner—four days waiting for in making preparatory arrangements to have a sufficient protective force to accompany, when all set out for Mobile—here reached, then, the sheriff in the buggy with him, then drives rapidly down one street, up another, and round the corners with a velocity that kept some three or four of the protective force in a gallop to keep up with the speed.

The reader will once more draw his own inferences. He will

plainly see that the principal aim again was assassination as the better method among outlaws of disposing of troublesome persons. The lying in ambush for one or two whole days on both sides of the morass, on both sides of the next river, the hurried rapidity of the return to overtake the sheriff before reaching Augusta, and the last effort to get clear of the "protective force" in the city of Mobile by forced speed through complicated streets; all these facts in connection are plain to the unprejudiced mind as to the ultimate object in view. Indirectly corroborative, there is another fact, which will be further noticed in the sequel, to the effect of one by the name of Cornelious McLamore from Kemper county, an important witness on trial, who crushingly and effectively broke down the testimony of the said Shoemake, but in all probability his life paid the forfeit; for McLamore from that time to the present has never more been heard of—his remains likely burnt or buried in some dismal swamp—another victim to the vengeance of the "clan."

Shoemake, the big dog among the band, this is the man, this the agent from the Governor of Alabama, from the Governor of Mississippi, employed to execute the highest of delegated State authority! If the then Governor of Mississippi can reconcile the rectitude of such action to his mind, the public is very far from approving the same. At the time the press from almost every quarter was loud in its denunciations against the conduct of the Governor. He must have known that the extensive ramifications of the Wages and Copeland Clan had produced a reign of terror almost everywhere, and he must also have known that the "confessions" had done more for its dismemberment and final dissolution than anything else; then why did he attempt to play into its expiring hands, against public sentiment and justice, when the imputed but misnamed crime of publication was done in New Orleans, La., and the author, who had only committed the "confessions" to paper, residing in Mississippi, and more especially while hundreds were satisfied of the truth of the narrations? However, from these revelations, the fact is made patent that wealth and a few distinguished persons can wield mighty influences against reason and justice; against common sense and the best interests of society.

## IMPORTANT INFORMATION GATHERED ABOUT THE BURIED TREASURE.

The order of events will now be continued consecutively from the time of the Sheriff giving bond and being released. Before the opening of the city court he was left with thirty or forty days to prepare for defense, during which time he visited Ocean Springs and a few other watering places on the Mississippi Sound, remaining a few days at Shieldsboro, now Bay St. Louis, and there made acquaintance with old Mr. Toulme and two other prominent gentlemen, who informed him that just after the publication of Copeland's confessions they took a copy of said work, and made a visit out to Catahoula swamp, in that county, in quest of the buried treasure referred to in the said confessions as having been deposited there by the clan for safe keeping. The map of this depository was lost during the famous Harvey battle, near Red Creek, in Perry county. These gentlemen informed him that they found the place as described by Copeland, and that every tree and line of demarcation as delineated in his description of the place could not have been more accurately given. They stated that there were three places of deposit, showing that in time there had been three kegs buried, which, from every appearance, indicated as though they might have been removed some eight or ten years prior to that time. The old keg staves and iron hoops were still remaining, and the perfect impress made by the burial of these kegs still existed, with a grown lining of moss which time had brought forth; on the whole exhibiting quite an antique appearance.

There has been much speculation and curiosity manifested among many as to who was the fortunate person who found this buried treasure. Let it be remembered that the Harvey battle occurred in some part of the year 1848. The description and mystic map of the place in connection with this treasure was lost in the time of this battle. Until the "confessions" were published in 1858 the public knew nothing about the buried money, but when they come out curiosity and opinion ran to an extensive height. Now this information was given to the Sheriff by one living in that section of country when the collision happened. He told him that a few days after the "battle" he found an instrument of writing which he could neither read nor in any way understand, and the same with all others around who saw it. To them it appeared more of a wonder and "puzzle fool" than anything else. He kept it by him for the sake of holding something partaking of mystery and curiosity. But having business some short time after in the city of Mobile, Ala., he carried this mystic paper along with him to this place. While there one evening on the streets he met with some of his former acquaintances. Thinking that this curiosity would amuse, he exhibited it for common inspection, and while examining and discussing the same, one by the name of George A. Cleaveland came up to peep, and requested to examine more minutely, when, after looking for a while, he folded it up in a very careless manner which then found a place in his pocket, remarking at the same time that it did not amount to much anyway, and walked off.

The person who brought this paper, not being aware of its value, did not care enough about it to make any objections to his carrying it away with him.

But the new possessor, in all probability, fully understood the mystic lines contained in it, and soon turned them to signal account. From rather a pecuniary condition of embarrassment at the time, as the Sheriff has been informed, he very soon afterward made an advertisement through the public journals of the city, expressing a desire to purchase twenty able bodied negroes and the like number of mules and drays, all of which he bought accordingly in a short time afterward, and more; and from that time to the day of his death remained independent, all the while increasing rapidly in wealth and external prosperity.

## THE TRIAL.

SIMPLE AND UNADORNED TRUTH STRUGGLING WITH ALL THE FORCES OF TALENT, WEALTH AND PROPPED UP FALSEHOOD—THE CONVICTION ONLY A VICTORY IN NAME FOR THE PROSECUTION, BUT IN REALITY A LASTING TRIUMPH FOR THE DEFENCE.

PRELIMINARY REMARKS TOUCHING THE TRIAL.

An error—a fault in the working of a machine, or in physical operations generally, is soon discovered and admits of very little discussion, as to whether all is right or something wrong. Too much friction, a cog broken, or some other mechanical defect in mechanical construction, and the machine will soon stop; and so of physical movements; a disease or some radical defect in the constitution is soon discovered by bad pains and bad health; and if no recuperative remedy can be applied, the consequence will soon be a death stoppage. But in the moral world, the difficulties are far greater and more extensive. Immaculate truth and unmixed error are soon acknowledged, but when deeply blended together, ages may elapse before any considerable or healthy progress can be made. In physical science, and in mechanical discoveries, the progress has been prodigious; but it is a question very much open to dispute, whether the world is now purer, better, and happier than it was three thousand years ago, notwithstanding the centuries of statesmanship and legislation. In *physical* realities, all appear to hail improvement with a welcome satisfaction, and gladly receive truthful discoveries, no matter from where they come, as if immediately experiencing a direct and general interest in all such demonstrations; but it is far more complicated in *moral* phenomena. Effects, either for good or evil, require a longer time for development, and are subject to influences from far more numerous and intricate causes, less

AUTHOR'S TRIAL IN MOBILE, ALA.—See Page 144.

capable of demonstration, and less capable of determining the share each exercises in the production of compound effects. Two persons may be equally honest, equally able, and equally desirous for the common good of the nation; but they will hotly dispute as to the proper means to be applied for this end; but if the opinions or theories of each could be immediately put to the test, and the results at once seen as in mechanical operations, a very different state of society would soon exist. If we could have a process of analyzation in moral transactions, so as to make the deformities of separated error at once manifest, and so with respect to the beauties of immortal truth, we might indulge a well grounded hope for rapid conquests toward the perfection of mankind.

Differences in organizations and in education, with vast extensions of clashing interest; these, when properly directed, may be rather a blessing than otherwise; but when allowed to run into the wildest excesses without any restraint whatever, the evils must be frightful in the train of consequences. The excessive philanthrophist is on for freedom, and will sacrifice every other consideration for the success of his ardent object, regardless of the reacting forces of despotism. The creature of inordinate ambition does not stop to consider who is right and who wrong—down with every obstacle in his way, that has a tendency to impede his ultimate design. The theological devotee prefers his own denomination to all others—his own all right—the rest all mixed up with much objectionable error. The individual who has made so much wealth, and attained to so great a height of pecuniary prosperity by means, no matter whether fair or foul, desires no change, even though it may be for the benefit of tens of thousands—his own individual or conventional interest will have more value in his estimation than the interests of united millions in conflict. Generally, those who have risen to honors, distinctions, and emoluments by the vicious elements in society, will spare no exertions which talent and wealth can command for the perpetuation of the same circumstances of public wrongs. But, it is true, where there are freedom of thought and action, public vices cannot accumulate beyond a limited extent before conflicting interests and passions will bring on the appropriate or temporary remedy; yet the victors not unfrequently, ere long, run into as wild excesses as their erring but fallen predecessors! so then it would appear that revolutions only amount to a change from one sort of excesses to another equally as pregnant with evils. Yet in spite of all these apparently vain and oscillating circumstances, there are underlying movements at work in the nature of occult causes driving on nations to either dissolution or a better and more enduring form of government.

If a government is so defective that it cannot sufficiently protect life and property; if its conduct is so fickle and uncertain as to destroy confidence and stability in the future, convulsion, decay, and death must inevitably come if the organic abuses are too great to admit of any other remedy.

Untempered liberty is worse than despotism; it is barbarism—might reigns and not right. All the passions of licentiousness are let loose, and the many weak are lawful prey for the few strong.

The idea which commonly prevails as regards frequency of elections being the effective remedy for all abuses of government, though plausible, is sophistry and the height of fallacy according to the lessons which experience have taught. It is all very easy and fine to contend for short terms of elections—all very captivating to contend that if one officer well performs his duty, he can either retire into private life with all the grateful honors of his country, or, for meritorious services, he can be re-elected for another term, all of which is the most powerful incentive to do right, and, at the same time, the most formidable barrier against intentional wrong. But what does experience loudly proclaim? "For the short term you will be in office, make all you can, scruple at nothing, laugh justice in the face, trample on the principles of rectitude, and you will be admired in the present and immediate future only as a consummate political trickster which may, without shame, be imitated by other succeeding actors. But if you mean to be honest, and tender of just rights and claims, with a desire for the common good of your country in rewarding meritorious services and encouraging the sources of true national prosperity, you will only be laughed at for your folly." These constant elections, as it were, open the store-houses for a general scramble, for a wordy warfare of frothy declamation, for abuse and misrepresentation of all the nobler traits of human nature—making virtue a crime and fashionable vices respectable. The most expert in business of this sort, are generally the successful ones in the contest. Before the excitement of one election is over, another more intense begins. Under present circumstances, no one can calculate with any reasonable probability of continuance of the present form of government beyond a period of four years while there is no security for keeping wild and inflamed passions within proper bounds.

Correct public sentiment, when free to choose, is apt to have a government of the same nature. Is it public sentiment that forms the character of government, or government which forms the character of public sentiment? Both of these considerations may be true. It is quite possible to conceive how a few intelligent and well meaning persons, commanding a sufficiency of power, can improve the character of a nation; and under other circumstances, *vice versa*.

We want a government sufficient to restrain the strong and protect the weak. We want a government competent to make good laws, and strong enough to execute them. We want a government determined to protect life and property, so that industry can be encouraged, and a confidence in the permanent stability of it maintained. We want a government that will purify the bar, and give a judiciary of competency and integrity such as will grace and adorn the bench for "its disposition to do justice to all." We want a government resolved to inflict punishment and stamp with enduring disapprobation any league or infamous association for the triumph of crime, no matter how distinguished or wealthy its members may be.

The particulars of the trial now to be given, is a striking illustration of the league for the triumph of wrong, in which not only the executive heads of several States were concerned, but also other high officials in power, with more of distinguished persons in different capacities.

As the caption states, their triumph was only in name. The retribution of truth and justice is sometimes tardy in execution; but, longer or shorter, it is sure to come. Nearly fifteen years have elapsed, since this trial terminated, and the public has remained uninformed to this day of the more important features connected with it. This long silence has favored the continuance of wealth, power, and the honors of office for the prosecutors; while the defendant was unjustly brought to the verge of ruin by the enormous expenses attending the trial. The phases are now being changed—one side going out and the other coming in—one recovering strength and the other experiencing decline and fall with reference to the future—consequences which should *immediately* have followed the trial, for if justice could be forthwith done without so much expense and delay, the evil perpetrators would soon come to an end; or, at least, would soon become diminished in numbers.

As stated in another place, the interval betwixt the times of giving bond and trial amounted to near forty days. One part of this interval was devoted to making preparations for trial; the other part was consumed in visiting on the coast with a view to gather such information as might be of interest afterwards. The information as to the discovery of the place of deposited money in Catahoula swamp is one link in the chain of circumstances which attest the truth of the "confessions;" another is the finding of the mysterious map in a few days after the famous Harvey battle, which is in perfect agreement with another part of the said confessions, together with the singular circumstances in connection, which were the means of George A. Cleaveland getting possession of the map, with other subsequent circumstances showing the strongest of probability that he not only understood it, but also succeeded in getting the buried gold from Catahoula swamp.

But the opening of the city court and the time for trial were near at hand, and the sheriff or defendant, had to leave the coast hurriedly to repair forthwith to Mobile. He arrived there some two or three days prior to the opening of court. He there found considerable anxiety and excitement prevailing on the subject. A number of collected friends from distant parts of Mississippi were there to be present and hear the trial, which was the general theme of conversation and speculation everywhere. Fortunate for the defendant, he arrived in time to summon quite a number of important witnesses, who were accidently in the city from various points on the line of the Mobile & Ohio railroad attending a railroad meeting. DeKalb, Kemper county, was well represented in this meeting. The delegates from this town all being men of moral worth and of superior intelligence; J. H. Gully, P. H. Gully, H. C. Rush, A. B. Campbell, Cornelius McLamore, and the illustrious J. S. Hamm, then presiding judge of his district, all from the above named place. In DeKalb, S. S. Shoemake had resided for a number of years, and these gentlemen from the same place were very valuable as witnesses in the estimation of the defendant; and, of course, he had them summoned without delay right on the ground.

### THE RECORDS OF THE TRIAL FROM THE CITY COURT OF MOBILE.

The Clerk of the City Court of Mobile has twice been applied to for particulars, or for a copy of the records of the trial. In his first reply the present Clerk freely confesses the records of the case to be misty, suspicious, deranged, and altogether unsatisfactory, without venturing any further opinion on the matter. In his second reply he confesses in still stronger terms, if possible, of the confusion of the records; important papers not on file; much missing; more deranged, and very hard, with any amount of application of labor to make anything of value intelligible for rigid comprehension—one case, Shoemake's entirely disappearing from the docket, and no circumstances or account left to show the cause for the same.

In substance, here follows an extract from the Clerk's replies: "I find by the Clerk's indorsement, that in the November term, 1858, the Grand Jury found bills for four cases of libel against J. R. S. Pitts, and four indictments were framed accordingly in the same term. They are found docketed, numbers 61, 62, 63 and 64, to be prosecuted severally by G. Y. Overall, C. F. Moulton, G. A. Cleaveland and S. S. Shoemake. There are four appearance bonds for six hundred dollars each, dated January 25, 1859. The writ of arrest is dated January 15, 1859. But the indictments are all missing. There is nothing here on file or on record showing any action of either the Governor of Alabama or the Governor of Mississippi with respect to the processes for arrest. The case number 64 has entirely disappeared, and no trace left to account for the same. In the February term, 1859, the trial of J. R. S. Pitts commenced on the 23d, continued through the 24th, and on the 25th was given to the jury, who on the 2d day of March rendered a verdict imposing a penalty of fifty dollars, to which finding the Court further 'ordered that the defendant be imprisoned in the common jail of the county for the space of three months, and on the non-payment of the fine and costs that he be further imprisoned until discharged according to law.' The case tried must have been that of Overall, 61, the papers of which have entirely disappeared, as I cannot find them on file. The two remaining cases, numbers 62 and 63, were continued from term to term until February 28, 1863, when a forfeiture of bond was taken against the defendant and his sureties, Colin McRae and James H. Daughdrill, and then continued through several terms to 21st of March, 1864, when judgment final was entered, and execution issued, which execution was ordered to be returned by the Commissioners of Revenue on the payment of all costs, the costs being paid by said Daughdrill said execution was returned. The matter remained in this condition until January, 1867, when the defendant and his sureties were finally released by the Commissioners of Revenue.

"The names of the Petit Jury who tried the case are Wm. B. Hayden, James B. Post, George Mason, George M. Brower, Edward Guesnard, John R. McBurney, W. H. Marchan, Henry T. Eatman, Walter L. Young, Benjamin F. Hunt, John A. Bevell and Wm. H. Vincent. The only witnesses I can find any record of are the prosecutors for themselves. The attorneys for the prosecution were R. B. Armstead, solicitor, and Anderson & Boyle, while Manning and Walker appeared to have conducted the defense.

"Imperfect as this history of the case is, it has cost me much search and labor to collect from the disconnected, confused and garbled materials left me for reference. The whole affair is a myth."

## COMMENTS ON THE RECORDS.

This communication from the City Clerk of Mobile is valuable in more points than one. In another place he states that there is in his office on file an affidavit from Shoemake relative to the prosecution. The nature and subject of this affidavit was not inserted in the Clerk's communication. Why this affidavit of Shoemake's as one of the prosecutors, and none to be found from any of the other three prosecutors, is a profound mystery. Again, affidavits before Grand Juries, in connection with prosecution for libel, surpasses ordinary comprehension. The missing of so many papers, and the derangement of all others, might be charged to the neglect or carelessness of the custodian, the then Clerk, but how can the legerdemain disappearance of Shoemake's name from the trial docket be accounted for? No reasons—no cause for the same can be found!

The present Clerk is bewildered, and can give no explanation on the matter. Such being the case, is it not reasonable to presume that the leaders of the prosecution then controled the files and records of the office to suit convenience? Prosecution foul in the commencement needs props, subterfuges and mystery in every stage of progress.

But the most impenetrable darkness of all is, Shoemake's name being found on the trial docket as one of the prosecuting parties. The order in which they stand on the docket is cases number 61, 62, 63 and 64, corresponding with which the prosecutors are G. Y. Overall, C. F. Moulton, G. A. Cleaveland and S. S. Shoemake; and in agreement with the same, four appearance bonds are found. The question now for solution is, did Shoemake really get a bill from the Grand Jury of Mobile at the November term, 1858, along with the other three? The files and records show that he did. Now let it be borne in mind that this man was the agent to bear the requisition from the Governor of Alabama to the Governor of Mississippi for the arrest of J. R. S. Pitts. Let it also be borne in mind that J. R. S. Pitts is positively certain that he never gave any bond to cover the case of Shoemake—only three, Overall, Moulton and Cleaveland's; and that before receiving the Clerk's communication, he never knew that Shoemake was one of the docketed prosecutors; but he did learn during the time of his trial, that Shoemake tried to get a bill in the February term, 1859, and signally failed. Choose either end of the dilemma and the difficulty is not at all obviated. If he did get a bill, the rascality is equally manifest. To go to Mobile, Ala., to prosecute while he was a resident of Mississippi, and J. R. S. Pitts also a resident of this State, is utterly incomprehensible in any other light than a flagrant outrage on every principle of law and justice. If he did not get a bill, the files and records show forgery of the darkest hues. So, then, from whatever standpoint the whole affair is viewed, atrocity and corruption of the most aggravated character stare the impartial inquirer in the face from every direction.

As before seen, the trial opened on the 23d of February, 1859. The indictments were for libel in three cases as the defendant understood the same. The prosecutors, first, G. Y. Overall; second, C. F. Moulton, and the third, G. A. Cleveland. As it had been previously arranged by them on the State docket, the defendant had first to answer the charge of G. Y. Overall. Had he been placed the last on the docket, the prosecution would have, in all probability, signally failed in every case; and even this first case, with all the deep-laid designs in connection, would have been a failure but for the extraordinary resources for the forcing of a verdict by foul means.

The design here contemplated is only to give a brief abstract of the more momentous features of the trial, because the whole given, would be inopportune in a condensed work of this nature.

### SHOEMAKE AND B. TALYOR IN COURT.

As before noticed in another part of this work, S. S. Shoemake will again be introduced as playing a very conspicuous part, not only on trial, but also before the Grand Jury, which was organized for the then present term of the City Court.

Notwithstanding the "records" to the contrary, the following information was given to the defendant, at the time of his trial, by one of the jurors himself. Shoemake, although an old resident of Mississippi, the defendant also a resident of the same State, and the work complained of published in New Orleans, Louisiana, yet he, with audacity enough, went before the said Grand Jury to get another bill for libel in favor of himself and against the defendant, but was sadly disappointed. This Grand Jury had had more time for thought and reflection than the preceding one, and peremptorily refused his application. Had he been unjustly injured, his redress would have been from the juries of Mississippi; but he had penetration enough not to make any efforts of this nature in Mississippi, well knowing that his character was too well-known here to succeed in making juries subservient to his dark purposes of crime and dissimulation.

On the day of trial, the counsel for the defence availed himself of the earliest opportunity to make application for further time, on the grounds of absence of material testimony, but without the desired effect; the Court over-ruled the application, and both sides were ordered to proceed to trial instanter.

While the Sheriff of this court was calling in witnesses for the prosecution, the name of Bentonville Taylor was particularly noticed by the defendant. This man, as was afterward learnt, had been conveyed by the clan from Williamsburg, Mississippi, and appeared quite unexpected on the part of the defence. His knowledge about the case then pending, could have been but very little or nothing at all, and was evident to all who were more conversant with the facts, that his presence there was not in behalf of justice, but for sordid objects of pecuniary gain.

The first witness brought to the stand by the prosecution was S. S. Shoemake. He came up with an air of boldness and majesty not easily described. Calm, deliberate, and with an external appearance of the perfect gentleman, he gave his testimony with elegance and beauty of language, almost sufficient "to deceive the very elect." His testimony, such as it was, was pretty much confined to a pretended conversation betwixt the defendant and himself during the journey together while under circumstances of arrest; to the effect that the defendant had confessed to him that the names given in the life of Copeland, were not at all reliable, and that the authenticity of the work was entirely valueless. This pretended conversation was wholly a concocted fabrication of his own to serve the ends of the prosecution. But the character of this man in a few more minutes elicited, will satisfy the reader as to what amount of credit his testimony was worth.

His then uninterrupted evidence being given, the next ordeal was his cross-examination by the counsel for the defence. The envelope alone, which at first contained the John R. Garland letter, was handed to him with this question asked: "Did you address this envelope?" After looking at it for a while he answered: "I believe this to be my hand-writing." He was next asked if he had at any previous time addressed a letter or communication of any sort to the Sheriff of Perry county, Mississippi. He answered that he had no recollection whatever of addressing a letter to the Sheriff of Perry county, Mississippi, who was then seated at the bar before the Court. The John R. Garland letter itself was next handed to him, with the request to state to the Court and Jury if he was the writer of said letter, which had been written and mailed at DeKalb, Mississippi. Here Shoemake hesitated and faltered considerably; and, in a moment, seemed to be fully conscious of the complete wreck before him. A transition so sudden from the heights of promising success to the most forlorn and abject condition of reverse, was too much for him to surmount. In this instance, he manifested a great reluctance to, or desire to evade giving a direct answer, but being forced by the Court to give a definite reply, he answered at last with emphatic words that he was not the writer or author of the John R. Garland letter. Now, for the succeeding and successful conflicting testimony.

The witnesses who had been previously summoned, were now called forth to testify to the hand-writing of the John R. Garland letter, as well as to the general character of S. S. Shoemake, as to whether or not his being a man of truth and veracity. After examining the letter, several of them expressed, according to the best of their knowledge, that the hand-writing was S. S. Shoemake's; and also, from his general character they could not believe him on oath. But another witness called for and introduced, Cornelius McLamore, gave still stronger and more decisive testimony. No man could have had greater facilities for thoroughly understanding all about Shoemake than Cornelius McLamore. He, without any doubt whatever declared the hand-writing to be, undoubtedly, S. S. Shoemake's, and that he for another could not believe him on oath.

### M'LAMORE FELL A VICTIM TO THE VENGEANCE OF THE CLAN.

This is the same gentleman treated of in another place, who so mysteriously disappeared the evening after the trial, and, from that time to the present, has never more been heard of. Whatever fate he met with, no one has ever been able to tell; but from all the circumstances connected, it must be almost certain to the thinking mind of all that he was cruelly murdered by the conspiring clan, who had so long maintained a sad career of blood and revenge, with all the practiced modes of concealment.

The following is an extract from a letter dated DeKalb, May 21st, 1871, written by a prominent gentleman and ex-Sheriff of the county in which the town of DeKalb is situated:

"There has never been any person living in the county by the name of John R. Garland. Mr. McLamore has never been heard of since the time he was a witness in your case, during the month of February or March, 1859."

Two powerful motives predominated for the termination of his existence. The first, the unrelenting revenge for the crushing defeat he gave to others, and particularly to Shoemake while on the witness-stand. And secondly, to prevent an indictment for perjury against Shoemake; for it will be remembered that he swore positively to the hand writing of Shoemake, who had immediately before denied the same on oath in open court. These two considerations, together with having just sold his cotton, the money for which he had then in his possession, will account for his presumptive murder. No one could better understand the hand writing of Shoemake than Cornelius McLamore, for, as the defendant has been authoritatively informed, the former was during some time book-keeping for the latter.

### G. Y. OVERALL PROVES AN ALIBI.

Shoemake, the first witness for the prosecution, had made such a wretched failure that no efforts were made to bring in the other witness from Missisippi of the same character, Bentonville Taylor. The prosecution next introduced two witnesses from Columbus, Miss., and one by the name of G. W. Overall, all to prove an alibi, and that G. Y. Overall was positively residing in another place at the time referred to in Copeland's confessions. This testimony was satisfactory and unobjectionable; but, as will be shown in further progress of the trial, did not in reality invalidate the confessions in any material point whatever.

The examination and cross examination of the different witnesses, with the arguments of the opposing counsel, occupied the Court for about two days; and had G. Y. Overall's object been nothing further than the establishing of his own innocence, he might have succeeded commensurate with his own unbounded desire; but what was he doing associated with such men as S. S. Shoemake and Bentonville Taylor? The complete unmasking of the infamous conduct of the former was anything but auspicious for the prosecution, and left a very unfavorable impression on all who heard the proceedings as to the character of the prosecution.

### THE ARGUMENTS FROM BOTH SIDES.

The closing of the testimony was immediately followed by the opening arguments of the solicitor for the prosecution, which continued for a considerable length of time. Next the argument of Hon. Percy Walker, for the defense, which occupied a period of two hours and a half in delivery. Distinguished as he had heretofore been on all occasions, this, as was said by his friends, was one of the greatest and happiest efforts he ever made. At the time the court-room was crowded almost to suffocation, and outside of it thousands were congregated to catch the utterances from his flowing lips. His withering torrents against Shoemake electrified the court; but his main argument went to show that G. Y. Overall had no right to prosecute in the name of G. Overall, and that it was another person referred to in Copeland's confessions.

The prosecution replied; and now the arguments from both sides being finished, the written notes from each, together with instructions from the Court were furnished to the jury, and it forthwith retired to its room for the purpose of trying to agree on a verdict. But it was soon ascertained that there was a very strong probability of it not coming to any agreement at all. After retirement for about twenty-four hours without any harmonious result, it reported to the Court the almost certainty of not being able to render any verdict on the case pending before it.

### THE COURT AND THE JURY.

Upon the reception of said report, the Judge made some changes in his former charges to the effect that if doubt existed, the Jury must give the defendant the benefit of such doubt; further adding, that he should not discharge until the rendering of its verdict; and at once ordered it to retire again, with additional information that if it required any explanation on any points of law involved in the case before it, to report accordingly to the Court, and it would give the proper instructions sought for. After the Jury had remained some day or two longer in retirement, the Court ordered it to report, on the arrival of which, the Court desired to know the points of disagreement. In answer, one of the jurors, W. L. Young, rose and respectfully addressed the Court, stating that a majority of the Jury entertained doubts; and as for himself, he had conscientious scruples as to the propriety of confounding G. Overall and G. Y. Overall together; while, at the same time, the principal part of the Jury did not believe that when Copeland gave the name that he intended it for G. Y. Overall, and that the latter had no proper authority for accepting the name of G. Overall, as published in the confessions. The presiding Judge appeared to be well pleased with the manly and intelligent conduct of the young gentleman, but informed him at the same time that the Jury must be governed according to the law and evidence before it. To this declaration, Mr. Young made the following reply: "Please your Honor, and suppose we do not believe the evidence in the case before us." This ready, but profound reply excited, to all appearance, a pleasant smile on the Judge's countenance, and created no little sensation throughout the court-room among the legal fraternity, some of which were heard to exclaim—"a pretty good lawyer himself." The Judge, feeling the weight of such an expression, did not attempt any further remarks in reply for this time.

## TAMPERING WITH THE JURY.

The jury once more retired. The court kept furnishing fresh charges in opposition to the first given; the last of which was so pointedly as to declare in positive terms that according to the law and evidence it, the jury, was compelled to find a verdict for the prosecution! Six long days and nights had this jury remained in confinement. Worn out by it and with excessive loss of rest, together with no hope of immediate relief, as the judge had declared his intention to keep it in strict confinement for an indefinite period, unless a verdict could sooner be returned; all these miseries endured, and in prospect to be endured, forced the jury at last to a verdict against its better judgment by the understanding or impression artfully made that it would be better to get liberty by agreeing to a verdict with a small amount of fine in the way of damages for G. Y. Overall, but had not the most distant idea of any imprisonment resulting. But the judge better knew the law which invested him with power to imprison for six months, but in this instance he sentenced only for three months.

In addition to the torturing process resorted to for the purpose of forcing a verdict from the jury in its last hours of confinement, other shameful means were made use of by outsiders of a tampering nature—such as the conveyance of notes and packages in bottles to that part of the jury in favor of the prosecution—one end of the string tied to the bottle, and the other end, in the form of a ball, thrown through the window to be received by the parties intended. The nature of these notes and packages could only be conjectured—the recipients themselves holding the contents a perfect secret within their own little circles. This information was conveyed to the defendant by eye-witnesses and part of the jury.

### SYMPATHY AND REGRET AS EXPRESSED BY SEVERAL JURORS.

After the sentence was announced, Dr. Bevell and others, who formed a part of the jury, openly declared that if they had been aware of the fact that the judge had the power to imprison, suffering as they were, never would they have consented to a verdict in favor of the prosecution. Another distinguished juror, W. L. Young, on the case, on seeing the defendant coming from the court-room, met him with all the warmth of genuine friendship and the most sincere of emotion, sympathy, and contrition, which will be best understood in his own words: "My dear sir, my feelings are deeply wounded, and I feel as though I have committed a very great wrong in giving consent against my better judgment—a wrong even to fine you so much as one single cent, and were the case to be done over again, with the light now before me, I would most assuredly act quite differently, for I now see my great error, though my greatest grief is that this lesson was taught too late to be of any service to you in your present humiliated situation." The reply was suitable, and in these words: "Permit me, sir, to acknowledge your truly sympathetic manifestations with all the welcomeness and gratitude which are possible to be expressed; and also to further express to you that notwithstanding this heavy stroke of adversity, I will endeavor to bear the same with philosophical fortitude, under the strengthening conviction that this is the most memorable epoch of life, and in spite of malignant persecution, justice will afterwards be done, and time will bring forth its appropriate reward."

## FAILURE OF PETITION— RECEIVES THE KINDEST TREATMENT WHILE IN PRISON.

Immediately after the sentence, the citizens of Mobile prepared and sent a petition to His Excellency, Governor Moore, of the State of Alabama, containing the signatures of over six hundred of the best citizens of Mobile, praying for the release of the defendant, but the Governor declined to grant the request because the petition was not signed by the presiding judge.

But the sheriff of the city. Hon. James T. Shelton, must not be overlooked. His conduct in behalf of the defendant was noble and magnanimous in the extreme. All that one man could do to alleviate the rust and monotony of confinement, was gracefully and cheerfully done by him. His friendship— his whole-souled treatment reached to an extent not to be surpassed by any. Hospitalities at his own mansion in profusion, a separate parlor well furnished with books of every description, and in everything else well fitted up in the utmost order of elegance and taste; no restraint whatever, beyond what the law required—having the whole limits, for exercise and recreation, of the prison boundaries; all such conveniences and comforts were freely and lavishly bestowed; and for which a lasting gratitude is due to the memory of the departed James T. Shelton.

Numerous other visitors, of both sexes, came to render all the comfort which humanity could afford. These visits were sincere, friendly, and consoling. indeed; in short, everything which could be done to remove dullness and make the time glide away agreeably, was done with cheerfulness and with

C—11

truly natural fervor of heart. Time did not hang heavily; but passed away briefly—a time which can now be referred to with pride and satisfaction.

#### THE CLAN GROVELLINGLY PENETRATES PRIVATE TRANSACTIONS.

The defendant, at the time of his arrest, was engaged to be married on the 22d of March following, to Miss Julia Pauline Bowen, daughter of Rev. P. P. Bowen, of Ocean Springs, Miss., but having become entangled in severe law difficulties, the appointed time for the consummation of this engagement was, from necessity, indefinitely prolonged. During this time, and more especially while confined in prison, the fact of such engagement became generally known. Malicious propensities could not be gratified enough by what had already been done, and by the little persecution then enduring, but the baneful malignity even extended to private and domestic arrangements. Some one in Mobile, over the signature of Amogene Colfax, addressed quite a lengthy communication to Miss Bowen. This communication pretended to have emanated from a female friend, the real object of which was evidently to poison and prejudice the mind to an extent sufficient to mar the existing engagement, and finally to break up all further considerations of the matter with a view to bring on a reaction of public prejudice to take the place of public sympathy, which was then running in favor of the defendant. But few have any adequate conception of the heights and depths of infamy which the clan could reach for the accomplishment of its infernal designs. But in this instance all such designs proved signally abortive, as will be satisfactorily understood by reading Miss Bowen's reply to a communication from the defendant while in prison.

It is very much to be regretted that the letter with the fictitious signature of Amogene Colfax has been misplaced or lost. Its appearance in this work would be valuable by the way of giving some idea of the clan's complicated machinations; however, Miss Bowen's reply will afford information enough to satisfy that she was far beyond the reach of influences which contemplated the ruin of both. Piety, firmness and devoted sincerity are conspicuous in every line of the reply. Let the reader now judge for himself:

MISS BOWEN'S LETTER.

OCEAN SPRINGS, MISS., March 16, 1859.
*J. R. S. Pitts, Esq., Mobile, Ala.:*

ESTEEMED FRIEND—Happy indeed am I to have the pleasure of acknowledging the reception of your kind favor bearing date 12th instant, the contents of which are so consoling and interesting that I feel entirely inadequate to the task of making the properly deserving reply.

This is the first intelligence I have had from you by letter since I heard of the last unfortunate results of your trial. Ever since the reception of this sad news my mind has been a complete wreck. Both mental and physical strength have visibly declined under the pressure of contemplated burdens which you had to bear; but the relief which this, your last letter, has afforded is beyond the powers of description.

In the first stages every effort was made to conceal a wounded heart, but in vain; the countenance of sorrow was too plainly depicted to be mistaken by those around who are acquainted with former cheerfulness. Laboring under pungent affliction from the silent meditation of your melancholy situation, none but myself can have any correct idea of the internal struggles with which I was contending. Under such a compression of the vital powers, earthly scenes had no charms for me; but the wings of last night's mail bore the glad tidings from you that all is well, leaving you comfortably situated and cared for in every respect, which affords me the most exquisite relief. From gloom and despair to joy and hope, the transition was rapid and sudden. The following from your pen affords a satisfaction which words are incapable of representing:

"You will please give yourself no uneasiness of mind so far

as regards my comfort and well-being. My friends here have situated me as agreeably in every respect as I could possibly have desired. Perfectly composed and resigned myself, I want you to share the same, if possible, in a still higher degree."

All of us, well knowing your entire innocence, deeply sympathize with you; and, as for my own part, this ordeal has only been a trial of my devotion—not knowing before the real depth of affection, which is now more strengthened and indelibly fixed on thee. *Fictitious signatures cannot avail, nor indeed any other cunningly devised schemes for the interruption of the peaceful concord which has so long been maintained between us.*

Even a brief narration of little ordinary simplicities may sometimes be enjoyed by minds accustomed to higher ranges of thought, and which frequently soar to loftier spheres of the grander contemplations of nature's wonderful works. Accordingly you will be disposed to pardon anything which you may here find apparently of a light and frivolous character.

There is nothing new in our village that could, I presume, be of interest to you, unless accounts of frequent marriages would have this effect. In affairs of this sort there has been almost an epidemic. We have had quite an inclement change in the weather for this season of the year. It is just now very cold, lowering, and quite unpleasant indeed; but the joyous cheerfulness manifested by the little birds indicate the early dawn of spring.

There is a charming lovely little mocking bird that makes frequent visits near my window—sings so sweetly, and seems to enjoy life with the utmost fulness of felicity. so much so that I am, in a doleful hour, sometimes inclined to envy the happiness which I cannot at all times share myself. Its warbling melodies echoing as they are wafted along on the zephyrs of the morning and renewed again toward the evening shades, sometimes excite peculiar reflections, which are very wrong to indulge in. I ought to be content with my lot, though it may seem rather hard, yet, perhaps, all for the best. The dispensations of Providence cannot be otherwise; and it is vain to repine against what we do not understand sufficiently. It is true my pathway has been interspersed with many difficulties and heart-rending trials from my earliest childhood; and they seem to still follow me up to the present day. But of what use to murmur? He who has blessed me with innumerable favors will do all things well. "He who has been with and comforted in the sixth trouble, will not forsake in the seventh."

I fear you will think me enthusiastic on the subject of religion, but hope not. All written has been sincerely felt; and were it not for the comfort of religion hardly one happy moment would I enjoy. Oppressed and fatigued, I can go to Him who hath said, "Come unto me and find rest for your wearied soul."

The family desire a united remembrance to you. Pardon error, and believe as ever,

Yours, etc., PAULINE.

### DR. BEVELL'S LETTER TO MISS BOWEN.

This is, perhaps, the proper place for the insertion of Dr. Bevell's letter to Miss Bowen. It contains important matter of a public nature, which will again have to be referred to in the subsequent comments which are to follow. Let it be carefully read:

APRIL 12, 1859.

*Miss J. P. Bowen, Ocean Springs, Miss.:*

Excuse me, an entire stranger to you, for the liberty and freedom I take in addressing you. Although, personally, we are unacquainted yet my sympathies are with you and your unfortunate intended. I formed his acquaintance in Augusta, Miss., while he was engaged in writing the confessions of Copeland—the cause of his present unjust imprisonment. Although he is in prison, and redeeming an unjust sentence, his friends have not deserted him, as is too often the case, but visit him regularly and inquire after his welfare with the greatest anxiety, and endeavor to administer to his every want and comfort. His friends, though numerous previous to his trial, have greatly increased in number since. We have made an effort to limit his imprisonment through the pardoning power of Governor Moore, by an article addressed to him in the shape of a petition, with about six hundred signatures of the most responsible citizens of Mobile; but in this we have failed, and, to my deepest regret, he will have to serve his time out.

We first drew up a petition to Judge McKinstry, signed by a respectable number of the jury, but hearing of his negative declarations on the street, we declined honoring him with the request.

Although we have failed in these efforts, the conduct of all the opposing clique strongly indicate to my mind that the principal stringent ruling is to gratify, and sustain, and retain political influence. The opposing party have by no means sustained itself to the world, notwithstanding the obtaining of a forced verdict and fine in the pitiful sum of fifty dollars, which the jurors are determined shall not come out of Colonel Pitts' pocket. The Colonel has the sympathy of the principal citizens of Mobile; and, among that number, almost, if not quite, the entire portion of the gentler sex; and as long as he has those amiable creatures advocating his cause he is free from all censure and harm. He was extremely unfortunate in not being able to prove certain facts on his trial that have since almost revealed themselves. I think myself they have seriously regretted the past and present daily expositions. Colonel Pitts is as comfortably situated as possible under the circumstances. He has the entire liberty of the prison bounds, with no restraint whatever on his person or actions—sharing freely the hospitality of our inestimable Sheriff and family. He has an excellent little parlor, well fitted up for convenience and comfort.

I was one of the unfortunate jurors who tried the case, and from my observations prior to, and during the progress of the trial, in my humble opinion he met with strenuous ruling and injustice. Yet he bore all with that fortitude and patience that ever characterizes a truly good man; and, since his confinement, appears to be composed and resigned to his fate. This has had a tendency to influence a favorable impression in his behalf among the citizens of Mobile. His friends in Mississippi, who are very numerous, are very much incensed against the Court, and manifested their indignation by public declarations in their public newspapers. His greatest grief and mortification are in your behalf. He suffers more on your account than he does on his own. He has daily the fullest assurance and confirmation of the kindest feelings of our best people. And what more could he want? It is looked on as one of those misfortunes incident in life that sometimes cannot be avoided honorably, and the only chance is to brave the storm fearlessly until a more congenial sun will burst forth to his advantage, which will be better appreciated and enjoyed had he never been in prison. I do hope you have firmness and decision enough to fast adhere in adversity—spurning the advice of those who would attempt to prejudice you against him. Sympathizing with him under the clouds of misfortune, rejoicing with him in prosperity, and yet be happy together; and may you both live, not to exult, but witness the repentance of your enemies, is the desire of your well wisher.

Very respectfully, yours,

JOHN A. BEVELL.

Miss Bowen availed herself of the very earliest opportunity to acknowledge and to reply to this valuable communication, in which will be found some statements well worthy of record.

MISS BOWEN'S REPLY TO DR. BEVELL'S LETTER.

OCEAN SPRINGS, MISS., APRIL 16, 1859.

*Dr. John A. Bevell, Mobile, Ala.:*

SIR:—I am in receipt of yours, bearing date 12th inst., and sensibly feel the loss of suitable language for a correct expression of what is due for your inestimable favor. It has been read with intense interest. It came at the opportune moment when most needed, and contains matter which to me is of the highest earthly treasure, and for which the ordinary returns of gratitude are but a faint expression of the true estimation entertained in my own mind.

To learn from one so competent to furnish correct information of the easy and comfortable situation of my much esteemed friend, Mr. P., is gratifying in the extreme. At first, imagination had drawn pictures too darkly of him being immured in solitary confinement where the cheering rays of solid friendship could not penetrate. How agreeably I have been disappointed. Your communication has completely dispelled for the future all such illusory apprehensions. Friends numerous, and sympathy not confined to narrow limits, with an abundant plenty of everything else calculated to alleviate the misfortunes of a temporary exile.

But allow me to confess to you that the recent trial, with its apparently sad results, has with me in no wise made the slightest change deleterious to the future interest and happiness of my friend. Previous to this memorable event in his life, with him I had pledged for an early approach to the hymeneal altar, and was fully satisfied then that he was, in every respect, worthy of such a pledge of confidence; and if his merit were deserving the same in that day, they are certainly, in my opinion, more so to day.

As yet I have not heard a single word uttered that does not fully justify Mr. P's action in giving publicity to the history of Copeland. The public good of his country demanded such action from him. Bearing in mind such circumstances, I could not, with any degree of consistency, suffer myself for a moment to be biased or influenced by out-siders, and, more especially, by those who are violently antagonist against the author for doing that which ought to be received by the public generally as a great blessing to society.

You will please do me the kindness at your earliest convenience to inform Mr. P. not to suffer himself to be in the least troubled on my account, nor to entertain any doubt of my unswerving constancy. In this respect, perhaps I am endowed with as much stability as any, and as much as he can desire.

Although heretofore strangers, nevertheless, I hold to be much indebted for the warm interest you have taken in behalf of my friend, and indeed mutually so of both.

Very respectfully, etc.,<br>J. P. BOWEN.

From every creditable source, profuse attentions had entered through all avenues of the prison wall; and now the defendant's time for which he had been sentenced was about to expire, preparations were immediately made to honor him with a "reception committee" to greet him from the narrow limits to the realms of liberty, where dwells the broad expanse of earth and sky. Confinement had not corroded the soul's finer parts; and to show how devoid his mind was of every semblance of prejudice or malignity, a brief extract from his address delivered on that occasion when emerging from his sentence bounds, will be read with some degree of interest.

AN EXTRACT FROM THE SPEECH OF THE DEFENDANT BEFORE THE COMMITTEE.

"Gentlemen, at this proud moment, the breath of liberty is refreshing. From an incarceration so unjust, you welcome me back to freedom with as much joy as I can possible experience myself at this instant of time. Rather as a very much persecuted individual than a criminal do you this day consider me. For this demonstration of your kindly sentiments, as well as on all other occasions, my gratitude is tendered in profusion. What is it that can not be endured while being surrounded with friends so devoted and sincere? The reception you have seen proper to give me, removes all doubts as to the manner I will be met by other circles of my fellow beings. Well do I know how hastily judgment is often pronounced without sufficiently discriminating betwixt guilt and innocence. This morning I leave the precincts of prison unconscious of any wrong by me committed, but, on the contrary, am strongly impressed with the convictions that I have materially served my country by giving publicity to the career of a band of men who, for years, held whole States in absolute terror. For this I have suffered, but do not repine, because *time*, the great friend of truth, must eventually triumph. From prison I come not forth burning with vindictive or revengeful feelings against any. Notwithstanding the wrongs endured, I have passed in my own heart an act of amnesty so far as private considerations are concerned, and whatever course may be marked out for the future, only the public good will, in this respect, afford me any interest for subsequent pursuit. To you, and to other large bodies of respectable citizens of Mobile, for petitioning the Governor for pardon, although a failure, yet equally do I return thanks for the best of intentions as though they had been perfectly successful."

Immediately after his release, letters of condolence and congratulations, from distant parts, and almost from every direction poured in. One in particular from a friend in Gonzales, Texas, will also be read with more than ordinary interest. Its spirit and intention were to impel him forward to higher achievements of fame and utility.

A LETTER FROM A FRIEND IN TEXAS AFTER DEFENDANT'S RELEASE.

GONZALES, TEXAS, DEC. 30, 1859.
*Dr. J. R. S. Pitts, Medical College, Ala.:*

"DEAR SIR:—In the sunshine of prosperity, friends will crowd around like bees on the honey-comb, but when the lowering clouds of adversity appear, there are but few who will not be found among the ranks of deserters, your case, however, forms an exception to the general rule. You have been favored by the benign and exhilerating influences of fortune; and you have also experienced the dark and bitter reverses with which humanity is so often saturated. At one time, she has thrown around you a joyous halo of felicity--at another time she has forsaken you with a treacherous inconstancy; but amid all her various phases of change which you have endured, the sympathy and good-will of every honest heart has beat high in your behalf. Your vile prosecutors succeeded by miserable subterfuges of law, which involved you in serious pecuniary embarrassments, and consigned you within the dreary walls of confinement, but time is now doing justice both to you and to them. You are mounting up into a brighter--a purer atmosphere of public estimation, while they are descending as rapidly into the dark abodes of eternal execration.

No one can feel more elated, or more disposed to congratulate you on anything pertaining to your interest, happiness, and success than myself; and certainly none more willing to contribute at every opportunity all within the power of one individual to your permanent gratification: how could it be otherwise? I have known you long; a chain of unbroken friendship has ever continued betwixt us; and more than all, I am proud in the contemplation that I have had some share in your early education.

Your attention is now directed towards the medical profession; and here I can express a few words of encouragement without acting derogatory to the principles of rectitude or sincerety; for if thinking otherwise, most certainly would I prefer the task of assisting at the risk of displeasing you.

The medical profession affords a fine scope for the developement of every faculty belonging to the human soul. Man, "the image of God," is the most wonderful and complicated machine in the universe. Here is the noblest of all subjects— vast, boundless, and inexhaustible. Here is a theme on which the finest geniuses of the world have been engaged: a theme in connection with which the accumulation of intellectual wealth and constant progression have been marching onward with giant strides from the commencement of man's mundane existence; yet but little hope—but little prospect of ever reaching perfection ; hence the encouragement for onward acquisition for further triumphs of science.

Knowledge is valuable only in proportion to its applicability for preventing or alleviating the sufferings of humanity; then where is the avocation more adapted to better accord with this sentiment than the medical profession? Of course, I exclude all consideration in reference to the many quacks, empirics and murderers, who assume the medical garb without the least sign of internal qualification.

There is nothing in all the wide diversified forms of creation that can give you such lofty conceptions of the attributes of the Deity as the study of man: Life's warm stream which ramifies and circulates in processes so wonderful; the numerous heterogeneous fluids which are secreted from it to answer all the astounding purposes of systematical economy with the nicest of all exactness; and all this by a "vital principle" which none can define, but which serves very well to represent our ignorance; the almost countless numbers of self-acting—self-propelling powers, with multitudes of valves, hinges, joints, all working in the grandest of earthly harmony; these are mechanical operations which belong to the Deity, and mock the proudest of all efforts in vain imitation. But what are these in comparison to the human mind—this noble prerogative of man? It is this which makes him the "lord of creation," and draws the broad line of distinction betwixt himself and the lower order of creation. It is to this we are indebted for the manifold wheels, springs and levers which carry society along; in short the moral transactions of this revolving globe owe their origin and continuance to its agency. The science of medicine comprises a considerable knowledge of the whole. To understand any one business well, we must have much information on the relation of many. The study of causes and effects of physical phenomena, as well as the faculties, sentiments, and propensities of the human soul, are all within your province. But without enlarging, enough has been written to urge and animate you on in the work you have so well begun."

The most remarkable action of any executive was that of the Governor of Mississippi in giving assistance to the "clan" in its expiring throes, whether intentionally or unintentionally, is not material now to enquire. From this action alone, but few are incapable of understanding, to some extent, the influence which wealth and distinction can exercise in cases, no matter how depraved they may be. This is only one instance from incalculable numbers which might be adduced where even the highest departments of State can be made subservient to vitiated purposes.

### A LETTER TAKEN FROM THE "TRUE DEMOCRAT."

The following was published in the *True Democrat*, from the pen of one of the ablest Judges in the eastern part of Mississippi, shortly after the liberation of the defendant:

Mr. Editor—We heartily sympathize with J. R. S. Pitts, Sheriff of Perry county, and are deeply mortified at the yielding course of our Governor in rendering him up a prisoner in obedience to a requisition from the State of Alabama. We look on this whole affair as being preposterous in the extreme. To have the Sheriff of one of our counties forced to vacate his office, temporarily, and to be taken like a common felon, and carried to another State, and there be tried as a malefactor, and for what? Why, for simply writing and publishing the confessions of a notorious "land pirate," one of a gang of banditti that has till recently been a terror to the whole country for a great many years. Such a course betrays a feebleness of nerve on the part of his Excellency perfectly unpardonable in the Executive.

The "Wages and Copeland Clan" have become as notorious in portions of Mississippi, Alabama, Louisiana and Texas, as was the pirate and robber, John A. Murrell, and his clan. It is well for Mr. Pitts that his friends volunteered to guard him and protect him until he reached the city of Mobile in safety.

Talk about rendering him up on a requisition that claimed him as a "fugitive from justice," when the offence, if any, was committed in this State, when he was a citizen of Perry county, and Sheriff of the county at the time, and quietly at home discharging the duties of his office. "Oh! shame, where is thy blush?"

But we rejoice to learn that his prosecutors have failed to hurt him. They may have forced him to draw heavily on his purse to fee lawyers, pay tavern expenses, etc., but they have not hurt his character. He stands to-day proudly vindicated as a bold and efficient officer before an impartial and unprejudiced public. Mr. Pitts is too well known in Mississippi for the tongue of slander or the hand of the bitter persecutor to injure him seriously. He is a native of Georgia—"to the manner born." He was reared and principally educated in Mississippi. And right in the county where he was principally raised, he was selected by a large majority of the citizens of the county to serve them and the State in the high and responsible office of Sheriff of the county; and that too when he had barely reached his majority of years. The intelligent citizens of Perry county elected him by their spontaneous suffrage solely on account of his great moral worth and his superior business qualifications.

The most amusing circumstance in the whole affair is, the report industriously circulated that Mr. Pitts did not write the book—that he is not scholar enough to write such a book. The report refutes itself by its own palpable absurdity. Everybody who is acquainted with Mr. Pitts knows that he is a fair English scholar, and a very good writer. The book is a valuable book; and it has done, and will do more to rid the country of the clan it exposes than even the killing and hanging has done.

Mr. Pitts may congratulate himself as having done more with his pen as an author than he did with the rope and gallows as Sheriff. Much more might be said in vindication of this persecuted gentleman, but this is deemed sufficient. Mr. Pitts is a young man, and will, if he lives many years, work out a character in high social position, and official position, too, if he seeks it. From his beginning, I predict for him a brilliant career in the future.

Very respectfully,     VINDEX.

### THE CHARACTER OF THE PROSECUTOR.

The vile character of the prosecution is not yet sufficiently understood. There is yet more to be developed. Enough has already been brought to light to give some idea of Shoemake, one of the main witnesses in the struggle to crush truth. Earth was never trod by a more dangerous and despicable wretch than this. He was the embodiment of all that was mean, cruel, bloody and horrible. How much superior the other agent and intended witness, Bentonville Taylor is, the reader will judge for himself from the following authentic testimony.

The statement will be remembered in the commencing part of the proceedings of the trial that no ordinary amount of astonishment was experienced by the defendant when Bentonville Taylor was called into court as one of the principal witnesses for the prosecution. The defendant well knowing the character of this man, he lost no time for getting the most substantial of testimony touching his notorious reputation. This testimony has been held in reserve up to the present period for reasons which will be given presently.

In Shoemake's evidence, the prosecution sustained such an overwhelming defeat that it refrained from calling up another of the same type for that time. As before stated, Bentonville Taylor was brought from Williamsburg, Covington county, Miss. The nature of his testimony, intended to be given in court, was immediately learned afterward by his card published in one of the Mobile newspapers. The substance of this card was to the effect that the names given in the confessions were forged by the defendant, and that Copeland himself was insane at the time he made the confessions, and the same entirely unworthy of any credit whatever either in public or private. It was thought at the time that Bentonville Taylor was to be used in the other two cases of Moulton and Cleaveland against the defendant to be afterward tried. This is one reason why the documents pertaining to Bentonville Taylor have so long been withheld. Another is, it is always painful, in the absence of imperative necessity, to make public such considerations as, under other circumstances, might be better enveloped in silence; but when charges of forgery have been made, and that the whole confessions are entirely unworthy of credit, then it becomes an absolute necessity to know something of the man who has had the audacity to make such charges.

First will be given some extracts from a letter which was intended for publication at the time, but on more mature thought was decided to be suppressed for the same reasons as just given. This letter is now in the hands of the defendant, the severer parts of which will still be suppressed for humanity's sake:

"Who is this Bentonville Taylor, where did he come from, and what his character as established by himself? It seems he came to Ellisville, Jones county, Miss., about the time or shortly after Copeland was brought from the Alabama penitentiary to Mississippi to be tried for the murder of Harvey—pretending then to be a Yankee school master seeking employment—having with him a woman whom he introduced to that community as his sister and assistant teacher. They obtained a school; he and his sister took board in a respectable family located in Ellisville, Mr. Parker's. They had not been there long before reports got out in this family of such a nature that is perhaps improper to publish. However, Mr. Parker ordered them to leave his house. The trustees of the school forthwith called a meeting, which resulted in the discharge of both. They were promptly paid off; the woman left for parts unknown, while he has been loitering around in the adjoining counties in a way anything but satisfactory, ever since. He got out a license to plead law, defended Copeland in his last trial, and then was brought from Williamsburg, Covington county, by the Mobile prosecutors, to there serve their purposes, in the most reduced of external condition and centless, but returned in the finest suit of attire, with plenty of money in his pocket —the rewards of his services in Mobile for falsehood and attempted deception. And this is the respectable lawyer from Mississippi, as represented by one of the prosecutors. A cheaper and more degraded instrument could not have been found in all Eastern Mississippi. A poor subterfuge to resort to such a man to lie men out of deserving censure. How readily it seems the prosecution knew where to place its fingers to subserve the purpose. A few more such licks will nail the truth of Copeland's confessions to the cross forever."

But read the documents now in possession, from the best and most respectable citizens of Jones county, about this man:

THE STATE OF MISSISSIPPI,}
   PERRY COUNTY.     }

This day personally appeared before me, A. L. Fairly, a Justice of the Peace, in and for the said county and State aforesaid, Franklin J. Mixon, who makes oath in due form of law, and on oath says that Bentonville Taylor stole from this affiant a bridle and girth, while this affiant resided in Jones county, Mississpipi, at, or near, Hoskin's ferry in said Jones county, in the month of March or April, 1858.

Sworn to, and subscribed before me this twelfth day of April, 1859.

                            A. L. FAIRLY, J. P., P. C.

Signed, F. J. MIXON.
C—12

STATE OF MISSISSIPPI, }
  PERRY COUNTY.

I, James Carpenter, Clerk of the Probate Court of said county, certify that A. L. Fairly, whose name is signed to the above affidavit, was at the time of signing the same, a Justice of the Peace, in and for said county, and that full faith and credit are due all his official acts as such.

Given under my hand and seal of said court, this sixteenth day of April, 1859.

JAMES CARPENTER,
*Clerk Probate Court, Perry Co., Miss.*

---

ELLISVILLE, JONES COUNTY, }
  MISSISSIPPI.

We, the undersigned citizens of said county and State aforesaid, do hereby certify that we are well acquainted with Bentonville Taylor, and know him to be a man of no moral worth as a citizen, no character as a lawyer, nor school teacher, and a man to whose word we could not give any credence for truth and veracity.

J. L. Owen, Att'y at Law, Ellisville, Miss.
J. A. Easterling.
Norval Cooper.
S. E. Nettles, Treas. of Jones county.
F. K. Willoughby, Justice of the Peace.
Hiram Mathas.
Isaac Anderson.
M. H. Owen.
Amos J. Spears.
Richmond Anderson.
Thos. D. Dyess.
John H. Walters.
H. D. Dossett, Ex-Sheriff of said county.

STATE OF MISSISSIPPI, }
  JONES COUNTY.        }

I, D. M. Shows, Clerk of the Circuit and Probate Courts of said county, do hereby certify that I believe the men whose names appear to the foregoing annexed certificate, are men of truth and veracity.

Given under my hand and seal of office this second day of April, 1859.

D. M. SHOWS, Clerk of C. & P. C.

---

ELLISVILLE, MISSISSIPPI, }
  JONES COUNTY.          }

I, E. M. Devall, Sheriff of said county and State aforesaid, do certify that I believe that the men whose names appear to the foregoing annexed certificate are men of truth and veracity.

Given under my hand and seal this 2d day of April, 1859.

E. M. DEVALL, Sheriff Jones county.

After Bentonville Taylor returned from Mobile, I saw him and told him of the rumor that was in circulation relative to his going to Mobile as a witness against Col. J. R. S. Pitts, and he denied emphatically to me of having any share in the transaction, and also stated that the aforesaid rumor was false.

[Signed.]   EDWARD W. GOFF.

The next question to be dealt with is the miserable plea of insanity, and forged names in the confessions.

First, let the report from the inquisition jury be read, which will be found on page 113 of this work. Again, it is well known by those who visited Copeland in person, that there was a keenness and shrewdness about him which distinguished him from ordinary men; and all the promptings given to feign insanity did not amount to anything but deserving failure. And as to the gratuitous charge of forging names, the defendant did not know anything about them previous to being given by Copeland. He did not know that such names were in existence before, and of course could not forge in the absence of all knowledge appertaining; but the conduct of the prosecution, with hundreds of living witnesses, go, as quoted from the letter just referred to, " to nail to the cross forever the truth of Copeland's confessions."

So much for the trial in Mobile in the first case, and now for the necessary comments to further enable the reader to comprehend the whole.

There were two other cases on the same docket of precisely a similar nature to the first against the defendant. For two or three years afterward he was in regular attendance, and always ready for trial; but the prosecution would not allow either case to come on until known that his presence was required in the army during the war; and then it had the cases called up, and the bonds declared forfeited. The two cases were ordered dismissed, and, some several years afterward, the bondsmen were finally released by the " Commissioners of Revenue" without injury.

Nothing is plainer than of the prosecution being glad of any plausible pretext for dismissing the cases—anything in the shape of a convenient opportunity for relief in the awkward situation in which it stood. Why so determined and successful to bring on instanter the first case in spite of the most powerful reasons for a temporary continuance? And why, when this was over, was it equally determined and successful to ward off the two remaining cases? Is it not evident, notwithstanding all the prostituted forces at command, that it was unwilling to make a second experiment? But how stands the presiding Judge affected in this slimy affair? In the first case, in defiance of the most powerful cause assigned in favor, he would not allow one hour of continuance of the case; but from term to term, from year to year, he allowed the prosecution all it wanted, regardless of all the urgent efforts of the defendant for the remaining trials to be proceeded with to save entire ruin from excessive and repeated expenses. But when the defendant's absence was compelled by demands made from the War Department, then did this Judge allow the case to be pressed forward by the prosecution, and the bonds declared forfeited! If this junta, or combination of Judge with the prosecution did not exist, the plainest of all circumstantial demonstrations are not worthy of any notice whatever. But this is only one instance out of a number, which will be given of this Judge's partiality—of his palpable efforts to do violence to justice.

Again, mark his conduct in endeavoring to obtain a forced and unnatural verdict. After twenty-four hours of close confinement, the jury returned with the report that there was no earthly chance of coming to an agreement. The Judge bid them, contrary to all custom, to again retire, with a declaration that he would hold it in confinement until the verdict could be made up, even though an indefinite period were required to accomplish the object.

Had he before been in consultation with the prosecution? Did he know the whole arrangement? Did he know that some one or more, perhaps influenced by gold, were resolved to hold out to the bitter end? And that one by one of the opposition, under the tortures of long confinement, must keep falling in to avoid further suffering, and more especially when the cunning device was resorted to for the purpose of deceiving the opposition by inducements to the effect that it was hardly worth while holding out when all could be so easily avoided by a few dollars of fine in the way of damages, which would not at all hurt the defendant? What was the meaning of the sham in his appearing, in the first part of his instructions, to lean to the defendant by telling the jury that if there was a doubt existing with it, the defendant was entitled to the benefit of said doubt; and then, in the last hours of worn out confinement, came squarely out in conflict, and positively told the jury that it was bound to find a verdict of guilty from the law and evidence before it? What was the meaning of packages and writing being conveyed to the jury by outsiders during the latter part of its retirement, or, at least, to that part of it in favor of the prosecution?

Notwithstanding the most justifiable and potent of all reasons in favor of the petition got up and signed by six hundred of the best and most respectable citizens of Mobile to be forwarded to the Governor for the release of the defendant, the Judge hearing of the same, emphatically declared, before being asked, that he would not sign it; and the Governor, because of this omission, refused to grant the prayer. Did the prosecution influence both Governor and Judge, so that the whole formed one compact ring to defeat justice? What says the learned Dr. Bevell on this subject—the very man who sat on this jury and witnessed all:

"We have made an effort to limit his imprisonment through the pardoning power of Governor Moore, by an article addressed him in the shape of a petition, with about six hundred signatures of the most respectable citizens of Mobile; but in this we have failed, and, to my deepest regret, he will have to serve his time out. We first drew up a petition to Judge McKinstry, signed by a respectable number of the jury, but hearing of his negative declarations on the street, we declined honoring him with the request.

"*Although we have failed in these efforts, the conduct of all the opposing clique strongly indicate to my mind that the principal stringent ruling and opposition are to gratify, and sustain, and retain political influence.*"

But the abuses committed by Judge McKinstry do not close here. A verbal copy of Shoemake's affidavit has just been received, the insertion of which cannot be omitted, as it will add new light on what has already been advanced on this subject in the commencing part of the trial, and will go still further to demonstrate the deeply sullied conduct of the prosecution and Judge. Let this copy be read with attention:

## APPENDIX.

[COPY.]

STATE OF ALABAMA, }
MOBILE COUNTY. }

Before ———, personally came S. S. Sheumack, who on oath saith that one J. R. S. Pitts did, within the last six months, in the county aforesaid, unlawfully, wickedly and maliciously, with intent to injure, defame, villify, and prejudice this deponent, and to bring him into contempt, scandal, and disgrace, publish and circulate in said county a printed pamphlet entitled, "The Life and Career of James Copeland, the Great Southern Land Pirate, who was executed at Augusta, Mississippi, October 30th, 1857; together with the exploits of the Wages' clan in Texas, Louisiana, Mississippi, Alabama, and Florida."

In said pamphlet, said Copeland is described as one of the leaders of a gang of robbers, murderers, highwaymen, and the deponent is represented therein by the name of "S. S. Shonesmak," as a member of said clan, or gang of robbers, murderers, and thieves; which pamphlet containing the aforesaid statement, referring to this deponent, is a defamatory libel, and is utterly and wholly false.

S. S. SHEUMACK.

Subscribed and sworn to, this 17th day of January, 1859, before me,

ALEX. MCKINSTRY, Judge.

---

TO ANY SHERIFF OF THE STATE OF ALABAMA:

You are hereby commanded to arrest the body of J. R. S. Pitts, charged by affidavit made with the offense of "Libel," by one S. S. Sheumack, and hold him in custody until discharged by due course of law, which may be done by any examining magistrate.

Witness my hand and seal,
Mobile, January 17, 1859.   ALEX. MCKINSTRY, Judge.

Received January 17, 1859, and on the same day I executed the within writ on J. R. S. Pitts, and have now in jail.

JAMES T. SHELTON, Sheriff. M. C.

---

THE STATE OF ALABAMA, }
   MOBILE COUNTY. }

I, P. LaVergy, Clerk of the City Court of Mobile, hereby certify, that the foregoing is a true copy of the affidavit signed by S. S. Sheumack, as also of the writ of arrest, and Sheriff's return, in a case of the State vs. J. R. S. Pitts, as the same on file in my office.

Witness my hand, this 19th day of July, A. D., 1874.

P. LaVERGY, Clerk.

---

### THE CHARACTER OF THE PROSECUTION.

Scheumack or Shoemake, all the while a citizen of Mississippi, the defendant a citizen of Mississippi, yet, he goes to the City of Mobile, in another State, among his friends and brethern, for process of law. This was changing of venue with a vengeance. With equal propriety, as far as law is concerned, might he not have gone to New York—not one whit more unnatural.

Sheumack, the "big dog" among the clan ; the man, above all others, steeped the deepest in blood, and crime, and dissimulation ; the man who brought counterfeit documents pretending to come from the Probate Judge of Kemper county ; the man who denied writing the John R. Garland letter on the witness stand, and whose oath was there invalidated to the satisfaction of all ; the man who bore the requisition from the Governor of Alabama to the Governor of Mississippi for the arrest of the defendant; this is the man to whom Judge McKinstry granted his writ to serve the purposes as specified in the affidavit.

This affidavit charges with "unlawfully, wickedly, and maliciously, with intent to injury, defame, vilify, and prejudice the deponent;" and again "this deponent is represented by the name of Shonesmak, as a member of a clan or gang of robbers, murderers, and thieves, which statement, referring to the deponent, is a defamatory libel, and utterly and wholly untrue."

In answer, will any one deny that such a "clan" existed? Will any one deny that its whole object was robbery, murder, and theft? It is presumed that none will have the effrontery to make such a denial in the face of such overwhelming testimony almost everywhere to be found.

The next thing to be considered is, did the defendant publish and circulate, with an intent to defame, vilify, and prejudice, etc., one represented by the name of Shonesmack, as belonging to the said clan?

Is there one disinterested and unprejudiced being in existence who can believe that the defendant could have any motive for "wickedly, maliciously," etc., assailing somebody he before knew nothing about, either good or bad—not even before knowing that such a creature was in existence? Up to that time, unacquainted with a single act of his life, can any one believe that the defendant published and circulated with a wicked and malicious intent to defame and prejudice somebody he neither knew by person or reputation before? Maliciousness can not exist while unconscious of any cause for the same. So much then for the unlawful, wicked and malicious attempt to injure the *fair fame* of Scheumack.

The same arguments will apply with equal force to the other names as published being the same as given by Copeland to the defendant; for to suppose otherwise would be the height of absurdity. The next subject for inquiry is, did Copeland, in his list of names, include Scheumack rightfully or wrongfully?

*Shonesmack*, and not Scheumack, was given in the published list in consequence of a typographical error. But Scheumack declared that the published name must mean him, and the same publication was "having a very deleterious effect against him in his own county, Kemper." Why was Scheumack so very sensitive? Why did he take on himself the published name of *Shonesmack?* Why was the publication having a very deleterious effect against him in his county, Kemper? An innocent man by the name of *Scheumack* would hardly have troubled himself much about Shonesmak. A man living honestly, honorably, and respectfully in his own county would not have taken any umbrage at all from the publication. Around here, there are quite a number by the same, or very similar, name, yet none of these complained against the publication having a very deleterious effect against them. Those who foam, and rave, and curse the hardest, are generally the object on whom suspicion falls the heaviest.

But this is not all, immediately after the publication of the pamphlet complained of, he wrote his John R. Garland letter, in which he described himself with the most perfect of accuracy as being occasionally absent for some time, and then returning with horses and mules, and other sorts of property which nobody besides himself could account for, etc., Let it be borne in mind that he denied writing this letter on oath on the witness stand, when the conclusive proof came next that he undoubtedly was the author of it. The counterfeit papers, with feigned authority from the Probate Judge of Kemper county, his several designs on the life of the defendant, with many other of his actions which are more than suspicious, all go to establish the fact that Copeland made no mistake when he gave his name and designated him as a "big dog" among the clan.

Ye, Governors, Judges and prosecutors, learn from the old adage: "Tell me the company you keep, and I will tell you who you are."

But there is something left behind of a still darker and more enigmatical character as to the mockery in processes of law belonging to the case.

Scheumack, a resident of another State, goes to Mobile to

prosecute for libel, and Judge McKinstry grants him the writ accordingly. The Sheriff is represented as returning the same to the effect that the writ had been executed, and the defendant in jail on the 17th of January, 1859. Again, the trial docket and the records show that four bills were got against the def'ndant from the Grand Jury the November term, 1858, marked cases numbers 61, 62, 63, 64, corresponding to which are given the names of G. Y. Overall, C. F. Moulton, G. A. Cleaveland, and S. S. Schenmack; and that the name of Schenmack disappeared subseqently without any order being made or without any cause being assigned for the same; and furthermore four appearance bonds given by the defendant are found on file in the office. In these cases, there is no record of any action being taken by either Governor of Alabama or Mississippi, the reason for which, perhaps, may be accounted for by the innovation and wrong being too great for Governors' names to be associated with on record.

Now, it is evident, from the affidavit of Schenmack, that he did not get a bill at the time the other three did from the Grand Jury of 1858, and it is equally evident that he never afterward got one; then why was his case associated on the trial docket with the other three?

The writ executed and returned asserts the defendant to be in jail on the 17th of January, 1859. What a farce! If the defendant was in jail at that time, it so mysteriously happened that he never knew it. A bond is found on file in the office given by the defendant to answer the charge preferred by Schenmak. What a farce! If the defendant gave such a bond, he never knew it—was never called on to sign it—never went before any examining magistrate, nor never knew, until a few days ago, that Schenmack had ever succeeded in any action of law against him.

Ye prosecutors, answer, if you can, how the records are made to show that Schenmack got a bill from the Grand Jury of the November term, 1858, when his affidavit of January 17,

1859, shows conclusively that he never got any such bill at all. Answer, if you can, how his name so mysteriously disappeared from the trial docket without any order being made, or without any cause being assigned for the same. Answer, if you can, how the appearance bond relative to him and the defendant is found on file in the office, when no such bond could possibly have been given. Answer, if you can, how the defendant came to be in jail on the 17th of January, 1859, when thousands positively know that such was not the case. If "something rotten in Denmark" is not found here, it is vain to seek from any other quarter.

### CONCLUDING SKETCH OF THE TRIAL.

Not in populous cities—not in the centres of accumulated wealth and misdirected intelligence that integrity and the administration of justice can be found. The highest functionaries of States have to bend to these rings and cliques. Honor scorned, justice mocked, and shame departed, what is there left to purify the national streams? Clans who live by plunder and murder can, with their ill-gotten gains, find plenty of law protection. Above all things, the Bench should be kept pure and independent, so that the criminal, though rich, cannot escape; and the poor and humble, if honest, can receive protection. Not as now, when judicial decisions are measured according to political numbers and the varied influences of wealth. If mercy is shown at all, let it be on the side of the unfortunate and those who have had few opportunities for improvement; and never on the side of those who have had all the advantages of wealth and education, and who should set an example to the subordinate classes of the community. Let the lessons cease to be taught and children cease to learn that because a man is rich no crime can hurt him; and if poor, though honest, he can be victimized by a snap of the finger from some influential person at any time. Is it any wonder at the increasing centralization of power? It is a necessary consequence under present circumstances. The corruptions and abominations have nearly reached the maximum height, and are at present of such a frightful magnitude that some remedy, ere long, must be adopted. Liberty abused must bring on reaction, sometimes for the better, but oftener for evils as great as those desired to be remedied.

And now, in concluding this sketch of the trial, which was carried on with so much absorbing interest and excitement, a brief recapitulation of its paramount features may be of some utility in bringing within our immediate view those incidents of it which are the most pregnant of meaning as to the future consequences.

In reviewing the conduct of the then Governor of Mississippi, McWillie, it is not charity, nor warranted by correct inductive reasoning, to suppose that he intended to assist the Wages and Copeland Clan by giving his approval for the rendition of the defendant as a "fugitive from justice," at the time he was an acting Sheriff for one of the counties of the State. It is, perhaps, better to suspect the Governor's ignorance or want of the proper information, than to charge him with evil designs. Had he known at the time the desperate character of Shoemake, one of the clan, and the authorized agent to make the arrest; had he known that the defendant knew nothing of the names prior to the confessions, and, of course, could have had no interest nor malicious motive to misrepresent, with the fact of locating the Three Distinguished at the risk of protracted trouble and a ruinous expense, furnishing a strong inference of the truth of all as to the names inserted; had he known that Copeland himself, on the scaffold in the last moments of earthly existence, acknowledged publicly and before living witnesses the truth of the whole of his confessions; had he known and reflected that the full publication of them must have, not only a direct and powerful tendency to disorganize the remnant of the clan, but also to prevent future associations of a similar character; had he known the full extent of the horrors, for years, perpetrated by this clan, and that numbers still living, from experience, can vouch for many of the facts as narrated in the confessions; had he known that an offense committed in one State or county, and the injury sustained inflicted in another State or county, the case may be tried in either, which gave him the right to use his discretion; had he known and reflected that the conflict must be between prosecutors—revengeful and experienced, wealthy and powerful, from another State, against youth—against an humble but honest citizen of his own State; had he known all these circumstances and maturely considered them, censure could not be too severely applied for his approving the rendition of the defendant as "a fugitive from justice." Who ever before heard of any person being dragged from one State to another as a malefactor on a charge of *libel?*

However, if he, without design, gave assistance to the clan in the shape of an unmerited expense and injury to the defendant, it is nevertheless true that he also, without design, was instrumental in laying the foundation for a more distant triumph in behalf of justice.

Many of the last observations are strictly applicable to the presiding Judge, McKinstry. We cannot believe that he had any affiliation with the clan, nor any sympathy for its continuance; but his reprehensible conduct on the trial can be better accounted for in the language of the competent gentleman who sat on the jury, and who had an opportunity of seeing and hearing and witnessing all, thus: "His strenuous ruling, strongly indicated to my mind, was to retain and maintain political influence with powerful cliques."

The changing of this Judge's charges, the veering about first from one side to the other, his expressed determination to force a verdict against the better informed and more respectable of those who formed a great majority of the jury, if it required an indefinite period of confinement to do it; and then, in the last hours of torture, came squarely out and told the jury it was bound, from the law and evidence before it, to find a verdict of guilty; and all this while knowing the awful character of Shoemake, one of the main witnesses, as proven on the trial; and while knowing that G. V. Overall had no right to prosecute in the name of G. Overall, when there were more of the same name in the place, and to which the jury believed the confessions applied as intended by Copeland; and more, after conviction, anticipating something righteously in favor of the defendant, this partial Judge declared his intention beforehand not to sign any petition for the release of the defendant from the prison; all these incidents taken together are too strongly stamped to be explained away. The refusal of the defendant's application against the strongest of reasons in contrast with his unreasonable granting the prosecution all it wanted for several years afterwards, is also something which will not soon be forgotten.

But it may be said that Judge McKinstry did no more than is fashionable in the present day—that of consulting political interest in preference to the eternal laws of justice. This is but too true. It is a deplorable fact that, from the most inferior to the highest of courts and officers, measures are gauged according to political considerations and wealthy favorites. Truth is sometimes very disagreeable, but it is nevertheless indisputable that when the progress is rapidly onward to idolize vast possessions under a system which rather favors than checks the spread of those evils which sap the very foundations of strength and national vitality, and at the same time, and in the same ratio, to dishonor the real sources of wealth—honest labor—the nation's decline and fall will follow in the wake of consequences under excessive government, no matter whether of Republican or Democratic. The baneful effects from either will be pretty much the same, as long as there are lacking the *will* and the *power* to restrain or repress excesses as they spring up. When general means of subsistence are easy, with plenty everywhere abounding, there is not much danger of convulsive change; but a prodigious increase of population with proportionally narrower resources to command, together with extensive disaffection and oppressive burdens from previous wars, then is the time for the exercise of prudence and a strict administration of justice in every department to maintain the life of the nation.

Granted that G. Y. Overall proved satisfactorily enough an alibi, that is, that he was not present at the time referred to; but it is again asked what was he doing associated with such men as Shoemake and Bentonville Taylor? Was he the tool of more designing men? What right—what necessity had he to turn prosecutor, when, as plainly elicited on trial, it was another Overall that Copeland referred to in his confessions?

The trial succeeded in nothing against the defendant only in crippling his pecuniary resources, and harrassing him in other ways. It rather strengthened than weakened the authenticity of the work. These circumstances, with the war, interrupted the sale for some years; but as might have been reasonably expected, truth can only be temporarily crushed to burst forth again with renewed vigor. Persecution only adds fuel to the flames.

Sick of the career of life which he had led, it was but natural for Copeland to repine against those who had shared his plunder and goaded him on to crime with ample promises of protection, and then deserted him in the last hours of his affliction.

The defendant could have had no conceivable motive to forge names—not knowing before Copeland gave them, that such persons were in existence; therefore, where there is no possible motive, there can be no crime or intentional wrong. So much then for the "wicked and malicious intentions," as charged in the affidavit of Shoemake.

The foregoing observations close the narrations of the trial with the circumstances of connection belonging; and now for particulars, as reasonably presumed, of another attempt on the life of the defendant in 1862.

Throughout the proceedings of the trial Dr. Pitts has been properly referred to as the "defendant." Hereafter his own proper name will be given.

### ANOTHER DESIGN OF ASSASSINATION.

In the spring of 1862, when returning from a professional visit, he was waylaid by two persons to him entire strangers. Just before the Doctor reached a by-path he was accustomed to travel, because somewhat nearer, he first suddenly discovered one of them near the main road, in a bunch of bushes by a stump, some fifty or seventy-five yards distant. The Doctor made a quick change of position; the rays of the sun fell on the bright gun in possession, which reflected a dazzling brilliancy for the moment. This extraordinary circumstance of itself was sufficient to cause well-grounded apprehensions of danger; and, accordingly, the Doctor kept a close watch for an excited moment. No sooner had he taken the by-path above alluded to, than he saw one of the two rush out—fast running through the thick woods in order to intercept him. The Doctor instantly turning his course, he at once beheld another person running in the same direction. There was but one available outlet for the Doctor to make his escape, and this through a long narrow valley with obstructing hills on each side. Both made a strenuous effort to get ahead of him in the valley, but fortunately he was mounted on a fine animal very fast on speed, which successfully enabled him to escape unhurt.

As before stated, these two parties were entire strangers, and never spoke a word during the whole transaction. On peaceable terms with every one in the settlement around, so far as known, there could not be a doubt on his mind as to this movement being another attempt on his life from the clan for the sake of vengeance for the past, and to prevent republication in

C—13

the future. The same conclusions must be arrived at by every impartial judge of the affair.

The following tragic accounts have recently been carefully collected from authentic and reliable sources, which, here introduced, will form something like an episode of after transactions of the parties whose names are also found in Copeland's confessions—transactions exactly of a character to correspond with the dark and bloody operations as given by Copeland himself.

### SHOEMAKE AGAIN.

From whatever stand-point viewed, there is something extraordinary about this man. He was particularly distinguished in the art of sculpture. He built the jail in DeKalb, Kemper county, Miss., which, when completed, was pronounced a master-piece of workmanship for substantial security. But in some length of time afterward, the report got out, probably from his own boasting, or some unguarded expression which he had made use of, that it was not safe. Inspection of the minutest sort followed, but not a sign of insecurity was discovered. However, when he got ready, he volunteered to show, and did show the defect which all previous search had utterly failed to find. He pointed to a place in the wall so perfectly concealed, yet with a very little exertion a vent could be made quite large enough for one person to pass out.

He was expert and dexterous in everything he engaged, but, as time developed, with an ultimate object of fraudulent gain in one way or the other. He was a scholar, yet this capacity only enabled him to attain greater heights of rascality with less liability of detection. Politeness, civility, and the most consummate of gentlemanly airs he could assume when his nefarious purposes could be best served by so doing. He was cruel, but not brave. It is said that the sister of his now brother-in-law received cruel treatment from him in youth; and for years this brother-in-law determinedly bore it in mind, and at maturity beat Shoemake unmercifully for the same. This is a case with one man that Shoemake childishly dreaded ever afterward.

But his wife, formally called Muggy Worbington, was made of different material. She was brave sure enough, which was sufficiently evidenced on a number of occasions; one of which was in making two men, who had before vehemently offended her, jump precipitately into the river from a flat to avoid the contents of a revolver which was too resolutely presented to be mistaken.

And again, in the malignant feud between the Shoemake and Fisher family, which culminated in a pitched battle with shot guns and pistols, near a brickyard, half a mile north of old Marion, Lauderdale county, Miss., in the fall of 1844, or early in 1845. Shoemake and his wife against Fisher and two sons, William and Theophilous. The fire from the Fisher family was too hot and severe for Shoemake; he left in haste and deserted his wife, who fought inch by inch with unfaltering fortitude until shot down by the greater opposing force with which she was in conflict.

Shoemake, before leaving Kemper county, made intimations as if disposed to divulge the interesting historical part of his life; and, at the same time, in reference to the tremendous disaster he sustained on the trial of Dr. Pitts; made significant remarks of a double meaning, but really of a nature to warrant the impression that the publisher of the Life and Career of Copeland would pass off this stage of existence, which would be certain to leave mystery behind for future contemplation.

Shoemake resided in and around Kemper county for a number of years. His conduct was always suspicious, but his address, his ingenuity, and his whole movements were so profoundly managed as to evade penal detection. Years had to elapse to fully develop the man for anything like a common consent as to his real character. It but required time to satisfy the judgment of all that he tainted everything he touched. And this is the man who was so sensitive because Copeland confessed him to be "a big dog among the clan."

## THE TWO HARDENS AND THE MURDER OF SHERIFF SMITH.

The names of the two Hardens were given by Copeland as forming a part of the clan. More about them has since been collected, which will now be read with interest.

About the year 1853 John Harden, from the State of Alabama, stole a fine animal, buggy and negro man, and succeeded in getting them safely to Marion county, Miss., where his mother resided. The Sheriff, Mr. Smith, from the county in Alabama where said property was stolen from, pursued Harden, and on reaching this State, Mississippi, he employed the services af Philip James, of Greene county, to accompany him. Finding Harden in the night at his mother's, he was by them taken on surprise, but made a desperate resistance, though being overpowered, was compelled to surrender. The horse, buggy and negro man were all found. Sheriff Smith had Harden confined within the buggy, and the negro man ordered to ride the horse. On returning, and when they reached the residence of Philip James, Sheriff Smith made no further request on Mr. James, and thought he could then manage without any further assistance. Accordingly they started, but shortly after they had crossed Chickasahay river the Sheriff was killed—appearances indicating that he had been beaten to death by a club. But whether by Harden or the negro man, none ever were able to ascertain. The buggy was rolled off under a hill. The horses and the two persons made their escape for the time being. Nothing positively definite, but the report followed that in some six or eight months afterward Harden was apprehended by Smith's friends, and by lynch operations finished his career by being hung to the limb of a tree.

His brother, also mentioned by Copeland, who married a daughter of Gideon Rustin, was hung in Columbia, Mississippi, about the year 1843, for the murder of his wife. Immediately after the murder, he made is escape, and got into the State of Georgia, where he remained for some months; but subsequently returned and gave himself up to the sheriff, but had not been long in prison till he broke out, and would probably made his escape, but was captured by some parties in a boat near by while he was in the act of swimming Pearl river.

John Harden was a powerful man, not only in physical strength, but also in determined energies and resolution. Years ago, it is said that he and Hampton H. Nichols, of Perry county Mississippi, disagreed—followed by a fight betwixt the two in the usual manner, and that Harden came out the best; although, for nerve and surpassing strength, it was before thought that Nichols had not a superior. Thus, one by one do the members of the "clan" drop into eternity by violent and unnatural terminations.

### JAMES M'ARTHUR, OR "CALICO DICK."

There are others of the "clan" still active and surviving. James McArthur—better known in some places by the appellation of "Calico Dick" still lives. By reference to the original history of the Wages and Copeland clan, page 89, it will be seen that this man became connected with the organization in 1844; and, at the time, was acknowledged by the former members as being directly concerned with others engaged in the business of counterfeiting money. Dr. Pitts has taken considerable trouble in tracing out the character of this man, and has received information from the best citizens of Mississippi and Alabama. Let this information be read with care and attention; and then, who can have the effrontery to contend that the names given in the "confessions" "are forged and the entire work unworthy of credit."

In former years, when the Wages and Copeland organization was in full blast, he was then looked on as a suspicious character and believed to belong to the clan, as well as having more or less to do with the counterfeiting business which had been the means of flooding the country with a spurious circulation.

This organized band of robbers, murderers and counterfeiters had become such a terror to the seashore counties of Mississippi that the good people of these sections were driven to the necessity of forming a "Vigilance Committee," for the better protection and preservation of society. By this committee, many suspicious persons were arrested, among whom was Jim McArthur. He, with a rope around his neck, piloted the committee to the swamp, where he pointed out and dug up the coining apparatus which was used by the band in coining counterfeit money. Here he acknowledged his identity with the counterfeiters, and was only released on his solemn vow to leave the country—never more to show his face in that region of society. Accordingly, he did leave, and was not seen there again until during the late war between the States, when he returned and was a great source of trouble again to all the neighboring counties around—committing more crimes of a more shocking and atrocious character.

After the close of the war, he again left that vicinity, and made his headquarters in Mobile, Alabama, where occasionally he was seen very flush of money. Also, after the war, he made a visit to Perry county, Mississippi. While there, he made inquiry after a woman, who had left her husband while the national contest was going on. The supposition is that he made her acquaintance on Honey Island during the war.

He is now well known to all this country as a renowned traveling gambler; and, among the fraternity of that class, is probably better known by the name of "Calico Dick," which appellation he received many years ago, according to his own statement, when but a youth, in the State of Georgia, for stealing a bolt of calico, and for the same received thirty-nine lashes. But particulars on this subject will be best understood by giving an extract of a letter from one of Mississippi's gifted sons:

"Calico Dick is the same brigand—the infamous Jim McArthur. He himself states that when he was a youth in Georgia, he stole a bolt of calico—was detected and received thirty-nine lashes, and ever since has been called Calico Dick. He was suspected of murdering a peddlar in Hancock county years ago, and acknowledged, with the rope around his neck, to the vigilant committee that he was a counterfeiter, and pointed out the apparatus for coining—confessed to horse-stealing and negro stealing, and had left his wife and children in Hancock county to starve or do worse. His nephew, young Frost, who kept a cigar stand in or near the Battle House, Mobile, was arrested at Bay St. Louis last year on the charge of murder, and carried to Alabama. I have not heard the result. McArthur was unquestionably one of the Copeland clan. He committed many crimes during the war. At any time during the second year of the war, when we had no law, if I had met him, I would have shot him from my knowledge of his crimes."

JACKSON COUNTY, 1873.

From another friend, in Jackson county, he still further exhibits the man in his true colors:

"James McArthur, long known as Calico Dick, has resided many years in Hancock county, Mississippi. Though absent frequently for months, sometimes for a year or two. His own statement when he first appeared in the county, was, that he stole a piece of calico, from a country store in Georgia, and being detected received thirty-nine lashes. So far from being ashamed of this exploit, he boasts of it, and when drinking often repeats the story of his filthy life. He soon made himself known in Hancock as a gambler; and from his frequent mysterious journeys, and generally returning with a fine horse and plenty of money, he became an object of general suspicion. The Murrell clan, and, subsequently, the Wages and Copeland clan were then operating thoughout the country. Negro-stealing, horse-stealing, counterfeiting, highway robbery and murder had been reduced to a system, and it was rare that anybody was brought to justice. If any party was arrested, some of the clan was always on hand to prove an *alibi*. Suspicion very often pointed to an individual, but people were afraid to hint their suspicions lest they might draw down upon them some secret vengeance—the burning of their dwellings or assassination. Thus, crime was committed with impunity. A peddler, known to have considerable money, was found murdered in Hancock, and though there was but one opinion as to who committed the deed, no one was arrested. The county was flooded with spurious coin. McArthur was known to make frequent journeys towards Mobile and to the Sabine on the Texas line, and when he returned, there was always an influx of bad money in circulation. He generally brought one or more strangers. Men of doubtful character, and with no apparent means of living, and never known to work, began to multiply, and this class was constantly around McArthur, and looked up to him as their chief. Though known to be personally an abject coward, he became, through these desperate men, an object of terror to the timid; and even respectable men were weak enough to court his favor. The late Col. D. C. Glenn would often say, after his attendance on the Hancock Circuit Courts, that he was shocked to see decent men jesting and drinking with such a wretch! The secret was that these men dreaded him and his gang.

Finally, somewhere about 1845, counterfeiting, horse-stealing, stock-stealing, and other crimes became so common; and the county so swarmed with idle, worthless, and suspicious characters, the citizens of Hancock formed a vigilance committee for mutual protection. It embraced the best, most responsible, and determined men in the county. They arrested a number of persons, most of whom confessed to being, or having been, members of the Murrell and Wages clans. The names of these men, and what became of them, can be given to you by some old citizen—such as Col. Claiborne, S. T. Randall, Luther Russ, J. W. Roberts, and others. Those who confessed to belonging to the above named clans, were to a man the boon companions and associates of the notorious Jim McArthur, alias Calico Dick, The committee finally arrested him. I have been told that nearly the entire committee was for hanging him instanter. Indeed the rope was around his neck; but some one suggested that if they hung him, many important secrets would die with him; and that it was better to spare his life on the conditions of full confession and his immediate and perpetual departure from the county and State. The cowardly and treacherous scoundrel clutched at this expedient to save his life. He acknowledged his crimes, gave the names of his associates, and piloted the committee to his camp in the Devil's swamp, where he fabricated spurious money. The moulds, forge, and a quantity of base metal were found there. The forger should have been handed over to the U. S. authorities, but he was permitted to leave the county on his oath (what was the oath of such a creature worth,) never to return. He left immediately for Alabama, where it would be worth while to track him. When the war broke out, and the vigilance committee of Hancock no longer existed—its most prominent members having died or removed—this self-confessed felon returned to the county. He appeared there, I am told, in the character of a bounty jumper or substitute broker, in which he swindled a number of confiding people. A band of his old associates returned about the same time, and during the war became the terror and scourge of the country. Some were deserters from the Confederate ranks—some joined the United State army, and deserted their colors came back to their old haunts and their old leader. Some were professional thieves, robbers, and murderers, who never belonged to either army, but took to bushwacking, and jayhawing for a living; robbed the old, the widow, and the orphan without scruple, and often added arson and murder to their robberies. McArthur was constantly on the wing on the old pattern followed by Wages and Copeland. Since the war, he has passed much of his time in Alabama; but I am informed by citizens of Hancock that he has for some months past been dwelling in that county. His doings in Alabama ought to be traced out. What he is after in his obscure den in Hancock county, will, no doubt, in due time, crop out."

Calico Dick is described by those who have seen him as having the appearance of being deformed from the effect of disease. The external appearance indicate considerable curvature of the spine. Others more intimate and better acquainted with him, say that this seeming curvature is caused by the constant wearing of a steel plate, which is used for the purpose of carrying cards; and that the plate is so constructed that he can without detection take from or add to his hand while playing, and with the assistance of his spring plate renders it impossible for any one to compete with him in this department of gambling.

The report of his death by being shot near St. Stevens is proven to be false. There is now a letter in the possession of John Champenoies, a resident of Shubuta, Clarke county, Mississippi, from Calico Dick, dated at Pensacola Junction, the 28th of May, 1873, and mailed at Whiting, Alabama.

There is another incident in his life which is rather amusing, and should not be entirely overlooked. In the year of 1868, he purchased a ticket to Enterprise, on M. & O. R. R., to Quitman, and got on board of a freight train, which carried him to the next station below, DeSoto, some four or five miles further than he wanted to go, and he had to walk back again. For this he sued the company, and got judgment against it to the tune of several thousand dollars; but the case was carried to High Court, and judgment reversed for a new trial. However, a compromise was made, and the company only paid him five hundred dollars, and gave him a free ticket on the road to ride afterwards.

Since writing the above, Dr. Pitts entertained some doubts of the truths of the whole of this story; and, to be better satisfied on the matter, wrote to one member of the company in high position, and received from him by way of reply the following:

"I know James McArthur, often called 'Calico Dick,' but know little of his antecedents.

"He did bring a suit against the railroad for taking him past Quitman to DeSoto, I think in 1867 or 1868, and Judge Leachman gave judgment on demurrer, *not a jury*, for, I think, $10,000. Exceptions were taken, and the case sent to the High Court, where the error was cause to send it back for a new trial. Before the new trial was had he proposed to compromise, and I did so for $500, he paying costs, but I do not know that he did pay, as he said he had given security for costs, and the Clerk might make them.

"I have not seen 'Calico' in the last two years, but presume he lives, and has his 'Tiger' yet. The last time I saw him was at State Line, where he told me he was 'flat broke,' and his 'Tiger' in 'soak,' and he wanted with his whole soul a ticket to Mobile on credit. He got it, and I have not seen him since.

"June 25, 1874."

There must be something remarkable about this man, otherwise he could not so long have escaped the last penalties of the law and the vengeance of an outraged population. The last heard of him, of import, was his visit to Escatawpa, Ala., a short time before the foul murder of W. C. Stanley, of this place, particulars of which the reader will now examine, as related to Dr. Pitts by one of the main witnesses involved in the case; but it should be first remembered that "Calico Dick" made a visit to Escatawpa, then left for Mobile, Ala., and in a few days after his nephew, Frost, came to Escatawpa. The current belief is that he was induced to do so under the influence of his uncle.

REFLECTIONS ON THE FOREGOING, AND ON THE CONSEQUENCES OF INABILITY TO REPRESS SUCH FLAGRANT AND WELL KNOWN CRIMES.

The masterly description of the terrible clans as they have heretofore existed, and as given by the natural as well as artistical pen of the Jackson county correspondent, cannot be overestimated. It will well pay for perusal and re-perusal again and again. Let the following quotations never be forgotten:

"The worst of human crimes had been reduced to a system, and it was rare that anybody was brought to justice. If any party was arrested some of the clan was always on hand to prove an alibi. Suspicions often pointed to an individual, but people were afraid to hint their suspicions lest they might draw down upon them some secret vengeance—the burning of their dwellings or assassination. Thus crime was committed with impunity. A peddler, known to have considerable money, was found murdered in Hancock, and though there was but one opinion as to who committed the deed, no one was arrested. McArthur, though personally known to be an abject coward, became, through desperate men which he commanded, an object of terror to the timid; and even respectable men were weak enough to court his favor. The late Colonel Glenn would often say, after his attendance on the Hancock Circuit Courts, that he was shocked to see decent men jesting and drinking with such a wretch! The secret was that these men dreaded him and his gang."

The above is a whole volume for contemplation. Decent, respectable, and distinguished persons jesting and drinking with renowned and scientific criminals through fear of conflagration and assassination. No efforts made to bring to justice—crime passing with respectable impunity.

Honor crime, and numbers will soon increase prodigiously. Make escape easy and almost certain, and the law will carry no terrors with it. Grievances, real or imaginary, and opportunities will be sought to bring in play the bowie-knife and revolver. Let life's warm stream flow freely, the sight common, and human life will soon be worth no more than the dog's. Let a callous indifference pervade the community when the tidings of outrage, robbery and murder are brought, and soon will the great arteries of a State's wealth and prosperity begin to languish and decay. Under such a system, can civilization progress? Will capital invest to set the springs of industry at work? Can wealth and intelligence thrive under such blighting influences of desolation? Is not government strong enough to protect its subjects? If not it should be, and the sooner it can be accomplished, the better it will be for all classes of society. Even affluent railroad companies have to bend to such men as Jim McArthur. To produce wide-spread fear and social insecurity, it is not necessary for crime and murder to be of an every-day occurrence; it is the hopelessness of getting redress from the courts as they are at present constituted that is so pernicious in consequences.

### THE HORRID MURDER OF W. C. STANLEY AT ESCATAWPA.

W. C. Stanley came to Escatawpa with a small capital, and invested to the amount of two or three hundred dollars worth of goods. On or about the night of the 6th of June, 1872, he was brutally murdered, and was not found until one or two days afterward, when the woods hogs were discovered eating up his lifeless body. An inquest was immediately held, and one on the jury by the name of Oye, tried to implicate a colored man, William Powe, on a plea of his having made some threats previously, but this insignificant plea was quickly ruled out of consideration as unworthy of any credit whatever, and properly so, for the colored man satisfactorily proved himself clear immediately afterward. A verdict of murder by some unknown hands was returned. However, one by the name of Frost began to get very uneasy, and left the place the second or third day succeeding. The passions of the citizens around became greatly inflamed by having such a horrid murder committed within their midst. And this was not the only one; no less than ten other brutal murders had occurred in and about the place within a very limited period of time. Blood and terror reigned to an extent never before experienced. To such a pitch of atrocity had this neighborhood got that no man could reasonably feel safe twenty-four hours.

Almost under any plea life was taken with but little hesitation by lawless violence. However, these good citizens held meetings to protect themselves against such diabolical outrages which then, of late, had been perpetrated in large numbers. They, well knowing Mr. B. F. Woulard to be a close observer, and active and energetic in every other respect, appointed him as the most suitable and reliable person in the capacity of detective to ferret out and apprehend the guilty parties. He obeyed the call, and, after Frost, took the first train to Mobile, Alabama, where, after much trouble, he learned that Frost had departed for Bay St. Louis, Mississippi. Still forward, and without delay, he very soon reached that place, where he found him stopping with one of his aunts, and arrested him almost without disturbing the family. There taken before the City Marshal, who was acquainted with Frost, and knew him to be of very bad character—knew that he had sometime before endeavored to induce young men of that city to engage in the counterfeiting business. Mr. Woulard well knew that Frost, prior to the murder of Stanley, was without money, and did not really have respectable clothing to wear, though, when arrested, he had two valises well packed with good, substantial clothing, which he had purchased when passing through Mobile, as learned by detective Woulard on his return to this city, with Frost still under arrest. Then and there, the firm of Jacobins & Brisk gave information to the effect that Frost had purchased from seventy to eighty dollars worth from this firm. It was now plain to detective Woulard that Frost had received money some where, and was required to give an account of the same. He answered by declaring to have obtained it by registered letter. On further investigation, it was satisfactorily shown that he had received no registered letter; and now finding it was vain to attempt to conceal any further, he was about to make a confession of the whole affair; but a person by the name of Cotton, in Mobile, stepped up and learned the cause of arrest, when, to detective Woulard, he proposed for Frost to be turned over to him for a while, during which time he would be apt to get from him a full confession of all the facts connected with the case. Accordingly, Frost was placed in Cotton's custody for something like an hour, when he returned with this report: "You have certainly got the right man; go now and arrest Oye and his wife, at Escatawpa." In compliance with such advice, detective Woulard lost no time, but hurried back with Frost, and there did arrest Oye.

But here Frost's confession should be given, which in substance, was as follows:

"At the time Stanley was absent from home on business, Oye availed himself of the opportunity by going to Mrs. Stanley, and by an attempt at strong reasoning, he persuaded her to leave him—all the while believing that Stanley, in such an event, would become so dissatisfied to an extent sufficient to cause him to sell his goods, which could be so managed as to give Oye the preference of purchase, when the money paid for same could be got back by a devised scheme of robbery. But in the interval between the commencement of the plan and Stanley's return, two Irish shoe-peddlers came into the neighborhood. Oye purchased the remnant of goods they had on hand. Forthwith one left—the other remained and boarded with Oye. Now, Stanley returned home, and found that his wife had left him, and his store, with all other of his effects, in the hands of Oye. This unexpected conduct of his wife had, according to Oye's calculations, the desired effect. Frustrated and discontented to an extent better imagined than described, he at once desired to dispose of his whole interest in the place. This was what Oye wanted, and quickly proposed to buy him out, which proposition, under the circumstances, was readily accepted. Oye paid the full value of the goods without any scruples whatever, and put Frost in charge of the same. Stanley, during the time he intended to remain in the neighborhood, and Frost now became room-mates, and boarded at the house of Oye. Up to this time, the progress had been attended with very little trouble, and everything seemed to promise continued success. The next movement was a secret consultation among the three—Oye, Frost and the Irish shoe-peddler, the latter of which, from inference, seemed to have before affiliated with such company, and likely his appearance as an Irish shoe-peddler at the time had all been previously arranged to produce the desired effect. This consultation was for the purpose of decoying Stanley out on a fishing excursion, so that he could be ambushed, robbed and murdered. Frost was the person agreed on to perform the part of betraying Stanley out, but, on more mature consideration, Oye could not repose sufficient confidence in the Irishman—entirely ruling him out, and broke up the first agreement. The next one adopted was for Frost to inform Stanley that Mrs. Oye had been receiving letters from his wife, Mrs. Stanley. Frost further intimated that he could so manage as to get hold of one or more of these letters, and would, the first opportunity, do so for Stanley's satisfaction. Stanley, very much wanting to know the whereabouts of his wife and children, urged Frost to get possession, if possible, of the letters the first convenient opportunity. So far, there was a mutual understanding between the two. But little time elapsed before Frost made known that sure enough he had succeeded in getting the letters from Mrs. Oye, and was then in possession of the same. Night being present, it was agreed for Stanley to retire with him, for the purpose of reading the letters, to a place some two hundred yards in the rear of Oye's drinking saloon, which place is a pine thicket or grove. Matches were procured, and forward they went to this designated place. Here Frost handed Stanley some sort of a paper package; and while Stanley was in the act of making a light from a match to a candle, Oye suddenly rushed up with a loaded revolver, and shot Stanley through the head—followed by five more discharges at him. After he had fallen, Oye was about to put his hand in Stanley's pocket for money, when a hollow groan was heard, indicating that the last sign of life had not departed, to fully effect which, Oye, with his pocket knife stabbed the victim several times in the breast, and then cut the throat from ear to ear. Oye now leaves Frost to get the money and drag off the corpse to some old well near by, while Oye would return and see that all was right outside. In this operation of dragging to the well, Frost became alarmed and left the spot.

The following day, Oye made a proposition to Frost to take an axe and cut the lifeless body to pieces, so that the same could be sacked and thrown into Dog River. Frost declined to do this from suspicion of a great probability of detection in so doing. As yet, no disposition having been made of the remains, a young man by the name of William Cooper, the next evening, found the decomposing body with active and consuming hogs around it. On the bloody grounds of the murder a pistol rammer was found, which was inspected by detective Woulard. Oye hearing of this circumstance, ordered Frost to immediately take the pistol to which it belonged, and throw the same into Dog River without delay, which was done accordingly. In the confession of Frost, he further told where the pocket book of Stanley could be found that had been taken away from him after death. Agreeable and true to his statement, the pocket-book was found, and contained a tooth, which on seeing by Mr. A. O'Donnell, was declared to belong to Mrs. Stanley—she having before shown the same to him. With it a piece of poetry, in the hand-writing of Stanley, was also found."

The fact of Frost and Stanley boarding together at Oye's house; the fact of the murdered body having been found; the fact of the sudden departure of Frost—before well known to have been in want of both money and respectable clothing, and all at once, found with plenty, and then his falsehoods and failure to account for the same; and then the fact of his confession about the pocket-book having been proven to be perfectly correct; these circumstances, with others connected, all taken

C—14

together, fasten guilt on Frost, and go far to establish the truth of the other part of his confessions in which Oye is represented as the principal actor of the whole.

Aware of all this when detective Woulard arrested Oye. He placed both under a vigilant guard for a short time to be controlled by Mr. A. F. Hooks. Immediately after the arrest was made, Mrs. Oye got an opportunity to speak to her husband, and was overheard to say something about a fuss, which in a few minutes followed by her using such language of obscenity and profanity against the guard which, perhaps, was never equalled from the lips of woman. During the disturbance, the intention was for Oye to get away, but the guard kept too sharp a lookout for the attempt to succeed.

The prisoners were conveyed as soon as practicable by detective Woulard, to St. Stevens, Alabama, where they had a preliminary trial, and evidence sufficiently adduced for committal. But all the while Mrs. Oye had been active. A writ of Habeas Corpus had been obtained from the Circuit Judge of the district, Mr. Elliott, requiring the prisoners forthwith to be brought before him for a further hearing. In conformity with the writ, the Sheriff of Washington county, E. L. Collins conveyed them to Mobile, and the evidence there produced was sufficiently strong for Judge Elliott to order them back to Washington county to there await the action of the circuit court.

When the case came up for trial, by motion of counsel, a change of venue was made: Oye's case being removed to Baldwin county, and Frost's to the county of Mobile. Owing to the great distance, with proportionate expenses, this change made it very inconvenient for witnesses to attend, by reason of which they were unable to be present in court, and the consequence was a discharge of Oye for want of evidence; but last reports say Frost still remains in Mobile jail—perhaps to be liberated also when convenience of time will justify; thus defeating the ends of justice and demonstrating the almost impossibility of convicting any belonging to the worst class of criminals.

Since the forgoing was prepared for the press, the following additional information has been received through a highly responsible source from New Orleans, La.:

### MORE ABOUT FROST, "CALICO DICK'S" NEPHEW.

"Frost shortly after the murder of W. C. Stanley, in Alabama, made his appearance at Bay St. Louis, with two carpet bags filled with fine clothing and his pockets full of money. He displayed this ostentatiously, and spent it lavishly in the coffee houses. While splurging in this style, he was arrested and taken to Alabama, on the charge of murder. When he was discharged (to the amazement of everybody) he returned to the Bay, and by some means was made an assistant light-house keeper on Chandlier Island: How he got in this position would be well worth finding out. Recently the keeper sent him to New Orleans to draw his (the keeper's) money. Frost drew it, and wrote to the keeper that he had deposited it with a certain firm in the city. On inquiry, such deposit had not been by him made, and he with the money disappeared some six weeks ago. He and his uncle are capable of any crime, but are cowards."

August 13, 1874.

### NECESSARY COMMENTS ON UNPUNISHED CRIME.

Talk of reform and State improvements, impossible while this system of things continue; "as well expect grapes from thorns or figs from thistles." Not occasional robberies, not occasional murders alone that poison the vitals of society. These will sometimes occur under the best government—under good laws and well administered; it is the ninety-nine chances for escape to one for conviction which produces so much evil. When punishment is sure to immediately follow the commission of crime, then society can repose in security; but otherwise, the honest and peaceable live in fear—the dishonest and disorderly in defiant lawlessness. Overt crime, regardless of law, with a determination to remain and risk all consequences from the farcical courts; in such cases, arrest sometimes follow, but the bail is ready, and with a few dollars acquittal will be almost certain. If the case is too dark and unpopular, time after time the trial will be put off, until, according to common parlance, the case is worn out, or some material witness got out of the way, and then the answer is "ready for trial"—well knowing the result which must follow. But, oftener, if the criminal leave the county or State, no more notice is taken—no effort made to reach and bring him back.

It is seldom that redress is ever endeavored to be obtained by process of law. This reluctance cannot be wondered at in the face of so many unblushing recommendations and encouragements from unprincipled attorneys in open court to willful violations of law; not to be wondered at when the injured prosecutor experiences nothing but abuse and malicious, or rather mercenary, invective, while the vile criminal is allowed to walk out of court unhurt and plumed with the laurels of victory, even in the worst cases which can possibly be conceived. If one person becomes irritated against another, no matter for what cause, either real or imaginary, he thinks not of investigation in the courts, but either sets in to break up his antagonist by private and malicious mischief, or he waylays, ambushes or seeks an opportunity to create a quarrel, so that life can be taken under the plea of justifiable homicide! But sordid, corrupt and sinister motives do not always stop at acquitting the guilty; they occasionally labor as hard to harrass and punish the innocent! The author's case, in his trial at Mobile, is one instance out of many where everything was strained to convict innocence. Sometimes one object in view, and sometimes another. Grand juries are not unfrequently acted on in a very disgraceful manner. One person, through spite, or for getting the property of another in some covert way, will seek an opportunity to get a bill from the grand jury. Another, to avoid paying a just debt, or to screen himself in some other case, for the purpose of producing intimidation, or, as it is more commonly called, "running him off," will seek to get a bill from the grand jury. Others, if the truth is too plainly spoken, will seek to command the grand jury for *libel*. Under such a system, the worst of men are generally the most expert in law, and always the readiest to fly to it to subserve their purposes. Alarming abuses in one direction seldom fail to be carried on in the contrary direction pretty much with equal proportion.

Lynch law is an unavoidable consequence of a mockery of civil law. No nation can long prosper under a reign of court corruptions. If the guilty, as a rule, escape, and justice not strictly administered, the sources of wealth will soon languish and decay. If the fashions of the courts are to favor the worst at the expense of the best members of society, the necessary results cannot fail to come shortly afterward. Under such a deplorable state of things, confidence and security cannot dwell. Suspicion and distrust everywhere; industry, the desire to accumulate, and also productive capital, will all be defective.

There are but few crimes which a determined and prudent government cannot suppress. Those aggravated offenses under the name of "Ku Klux" depredations, how soon they were put down under a vigorous execution of law. If the government of this State continues as it has begun, there will be no more of dueling, or at least so rare as not to be productive of much injury. The certainty of punishment, even in rare cases, will relieve society from serious harm on this account.

States, Empires and Republics search for the first causes of their decline and fall, and they will be found to consist in the vitiated customs of the rulers in the various departments of governments, in a reckless trampling on the principles of justice without shame, without remorse, and, above all, in overgrown corruptions practiced with the honors of emoluments and distinctions.

## CONCLUSION.

And now it is only necessary to add, in reference to the Wages and Copeland Clan, as an organization, it is broken up, though isolated individuals who belonged to it still continue to perpetrate crime whenever anything like a favorable opportunity offers. For a lengthy duration of time this clan spread terror and desolation both far and wide. Happily for present society, as an organized body, it is numbered on the dark and bloody pages of the past.

The publication of the confessions by the author was productive of much good. The high and mighty outside aiders severely felt the blows. But for the support given by such auxilary aiders the organization would have come to dissolution much earlier. It is such influential aiders and abettors, in warding off the chains of law, which give vitality to movements of this character. The decline began from the death of the President and leader, Wages, and also at the same time the death of the preaching hypocrite, McGrath. This change was further accelerated by the execution of Copeland, and the narrow escape of another brother, together with the publication of the confessions, laying open to public gaze the implicated parties and the principal movement of the whole.

But the expiration of one sort of lawlessness does not preclude the existence of others more dangerous, because more subtle and more in accordance with the corruptions in the high departments of States, and more in harmony with the operations of those who boldly trample on rectitude and the laws of the nation. Rings and cliques are not confined to political considerations alone, but descend to many other important affairs of life. A union of an inferior and unprincipled lawyer with a subordinate officer, and these again with a league of reckless and desperate "strikers," who can make money almost at any time from the honest earnings of the less expert, and all by forms and processes of law. This is one class of rings compla'ned of, the evils from which are of a frightful magnitude. They weave the net, goad the honest but unwary into its meshes, and revel on the spoils which have been extorted from litigation. The former modes of robbery, plunder and murder have, to a great extent, been superceded by, if possible, worse evils in the form of a science as taught and practiced by these rings and cliques. Crimes which formerly had to encounter hard-ships and danger, can now be accomplished by other means with honors, profits, and a plausible sanction of law. Government should have power sufficient to be able and willing to crush such proceedings, which, unchecked, must, ere long, produce another national convulsion.

Copeland's crimes were huge and many. Before he had reached the meridian of life he paid the last and highest penalty of the law. He was cut down anterior to the attainment of the flower of his days—a melancholy example to all who prefer robbery and murder to the honest and peaceful pursuits of industry. With all the weight of crime belonging, he made some atonement by his valuable confessions in the last hours of his existence. It is not clear what were the actuating motives; whether smarting under disappointment, and goaded on by a spirit of revenge against those who had promised him safety and protection, but did not prevent him enduring years of imprisonment with the immediate prospect of a violent and ignominious death, or sick of life, with no hope of earthly relief, and oppressed with painful reflections on the past—conscious that the affairs of this world could not concern him but a few days longer—it is more than probable that the task of disclosing the dreadful operations of his past life in associations with others, afforded him some repose or satisfaction in the unhappy situation he was then placed. With some, in the condition of distress and despair, there is perhaps nothing which can give a greater temporary relief than for the mind to be intensely fixed and engaged on something which is to live after the body has finished its earthly career.

No matter in what way the confessions may be put to the test, they come out of the ordeal firmer and stronger than before. They cannot be broken down in the severest conflicts in organized courts for the purpose. A partisan Judge, supported by a phalanx of talent and wealth, with all other influences brought to bear, cannot, as has been tried, destroy nor impair the invulnerable facts which they contain. Search for internal evidences of truth, and they will be found in ample profusion. Appeal to the last testimony of a dying man on the scaffold, and it fully confirms the correctness of his confessions as made some short time before. Ask numbers of still living witnesses, and they will vouch for the substantial accuracy of the facts as related in these confessions. Call in time, the great arbiter of disputes, and the revelations since made all go to corroborate the validity of the work so obnoxious to the guilty implicated in it.

If there are such occurrences as *special* acts of Providence, the author of this work has certainly been favored. The numerous snares set, the manifold plots laid for his life—these considered and understood, and it is more than marvelous how he has so far escaped destruction. Many devoted friends have endeavored to dissuade him from the present object of publication, because of the dangerous elements in high life which affect society, but, for life or death, "the die is cast." The confidence in Providence, in prudence, and in the better portions of society give him hope—conscious that whatever fate the body may meet, truth will survive.

Long associations, official position, and many other causes may prevent abler minds from grasping the evils which have been only faintly touched on in this humble and unostentatious work which is now submitted to the public. The thunders and turbulent billows of criticism may play in wild warfare against it, but simplicity and truth will finally prove more than the match to sustain it.

The author has studiously avoided tinting any of his observations with preferences in favor of either of the conflicting political parties of the day. He has indulged in no personal considerations for the sake of revenge. He has constantly kept in view public evils as they at present exist, and can see no effective remedy from the triumph of either of the political parties. The evils are fundamental, and require new combinations to meet the exegencies of the times, and to prevent further of intestine convulsion.

In concentrating, or giving additional *power*, the secret and difficulty consist in preventing the *abuse* of this power. Not in excessively frequent elections; not in the glowing descriptions as given by Republican and Democratic orators and writers, which have had their origin in the wild domains of fancy; nor not in the harsh acerbitude which come from the archieves of despotism can the remedy be found to prevent the abuse of power. All these have sufficiently been tried with a melancholy failure. A form of government perhaps well adapted to one stage in the progress of a nation, may, if continued, prove fatal in a more advanced period of progression.

Let us hope that passions will subside within due bounds for temperate reasons to mount the throne, so that this necessary change can be accomplished without further effusions of blood —resulting in permanent order, peace and prosperity for the enjoyment of every class in this great and powerful nation.

C—15

# INDEX.

|  | PAGE. |
|---|---|
| Memoir of the Author.... | 3 |
| Introduction................ | 5 |
| Hon. T. C. Carter's Certificate. | 12 |
| Preface.. | 19 |
| Life and Career of James Copeland... | 21 |
| Poisoning the Overseer in Texas.... | 37 |
| Murder of two Mexicans in Texas...... | 41 |
| Welter and Harden—Welter acting as U. S. Marshal..... | 64 |
| Plot to kill Robert Lott and Thos. Sumrall............. | 66 |
| Mr. Moore in pursuit of the Hypocrite Preacher McGrath | 68 |
| McGrath in Disguise................ | 76 |
| Murder of O'Conner on the Mississippi River..... | 77 |
| Meeting of the Clan in Mobile, Ala................... | 88 |
| Burning of Eli Moffitt's House and attempted Murder of his Wife............. | 96 |
| Wages and McGrath killed by Harvey | 99 |
| The Famous Harvey Battle............. | 103 |
| Trial of James Copeland................ | 110 |
| Execution................ | 118 |
| Members of the Copeland Clan................ | 120 |
| Copeland's Letter to his Mother.... | 121 |
| Mystic Alphabet.... | 122 |

## APPENDIX.

|  |  |
|---|---|
| S. S. Shoemake and his John R. Garland Letter......... | 127 |
| Sheriff's reply..... | 129 |

|  | PAGE. |
|---|---|
| S. S. Shoemake visits the Sheriff... | 130 |
| Shoemake returns with a writ for the arrest of the Sheriff | 133 |
| Important information about the buried money........ | 142 |
| The Trial in Mobile, Ala.................. | 144 |
| The Records of the Trial from the City Court of Mobile.. | 149 |
| Comments on the Records ....... | 151 |
| Shoemake and B. Taylor in Court.... | 153 |
| McLamore fell a victim to the vengeance of the Clan.. | 156 |
| G. Y. Overall, proves an alibi...... | 157 |
| The Court and the Jury........... | 158 |
| Tampering with the Jury........... | 159 |
| Sympathy of the Jury... | 160 |
| Failure of Petition..... | 161 |
| Miss Bowen's Letter.... | 163 |
| Dr. Beveil's Letter to Miss Bowen............... | 165 |
| Miss Bowen's Reply................... | 167 |
| An Extract from the speech of the Defendant before the Committee.... | 169 |
| A Letter from Gonzales, Texas, to Defendant.... | 170 |
| A Letter taken from the "True Democrat"......... | 173 |
| Character of the Prosecution........ | 175 |
| Concluding Sketch of the Trial..... | 188 |
| Another design of assassination.... | 193 |
| Shoemake again..... | 194 |
| The murder of Sheriff Smith, of Alabama............ | 196 |
| James McArthur, or "Calico Dick"................ | 197 |
| Reflections on the history of "Calico Dick"............ | 203 |
| The horried murder of W. C. Stanley, at Escatawpa, Ala.. | 205 |
| Necessary comments on unpunished crime..... ......... | 211 |

www.ingramcontent.com/pod-product-compliance
Lightning Source LLC
Chambersburg PA
CBHW021839230426
43669CB00008B/1023